CONTENTS

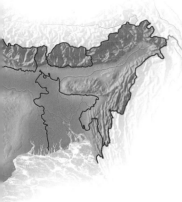

HOW TO USE THIS ATLAS 4
EARTH FACTS 5
COUNTRIES OF THE WORLD 6-7
SCANDINAVIA AND FINLAND 8-9
LOW COUNTRIES 1C-11
BRITISH ISLES 12-13
FRANCE AND MONACO 14-15
GERMANY 16-17
IBERIAN PENINSULA 18-19
ITALY AND THE ALPS 20-21
CENTRAL EUROPE 22-23
BALKANS AND ROMANIA 24-25
RUSSIA AND ITS NEIGHBOURS 26-27
CANADA 28-29
USA 30-33
MEXICO, CENTRAL AMERICA AND 34-35
THE CARIBBEAN
NORTH ANDEAN COUNTRIES 36-37
BRAZIL AND ITS NEIGHBOURS 38-39
ARGENTINA AND ITS NEIGHBOURS 40-41
SOUTHWEST ASIA 42-43
INDIA AND ITS NEIGHBOURS 44-45
CHINA AND ITS NEIGHBOURS 46-47
JAPAN 48-49
SOUTHEAST ASIA 50-51
NORTH AND WEST AFRICA 52-53
CENTRAL, EASTERN AND SOUTHERN AFRICA 54-55
AUSTRALIA 56-57
NEW ZEALAND AND THE PACIFIC 58-59
POLAR LANDS 60
INDEX 61-64

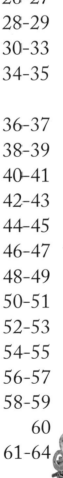
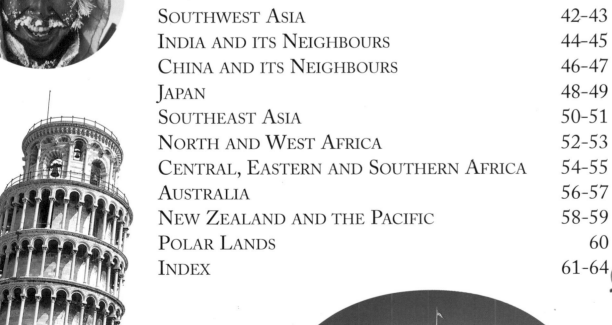

HOW TO USE THIS ATLAS

WELCOME TO THE PLANET EARTH! This atlas shows you the world we live in. An atlas is any large book of maps. Maps are plans which show the surface of a planet as if it was flat, instead of round. They show the lie of the land, the rivers and coastlines, mountains and seas.

Maps which just show the details of the landscape are called 'physical'. Maps which just show the borders of countries, states, counties or provinces are called 'political'. The maps in this book show the physical details of the land, but they show national borders and major cities as well. Maps use signs and symbols to give you more information. Look at the key to find out what they mean.

So how do you find the city or country you are looking for? First of all look up the name you want in the index on p.61. When you have found the right page, look for the name on the big map of the region. Next to each regional map, look for the little map which helps you to see at a glance which part of the world is being shown.

Next, read the words to find out more about the countries, the climate of the region, the peoples and how they live. Small boxes also give you key facts and figures about each of the countries. They tell you the area, the population size, the name of the capital city, the country's official language or languages and the currency, or type of money, used by the people there.

When you read about distant lands, it may help to compare them with where you live. Are they bigger or smaller, hotter or wetter, more crowded? You might use the maps to do a bit of detective work. Can you work out why most Australian cities are near the coast, or why most Canadian cities are in the south of the country?

Coastlines and borders

The borders of Japan are natural, because the country is made up of islands. Other countries may have land borders, marked by a line on the map.

Colours

On this map the different colours show you at a glance the physical features of the landscape. Each colour represents a type of geographic feature.

Spot the mountain

This symbol means 'mountain'. The mountain's name is printed next to it, along with the height of the summit above sea level. The height is given in metres.

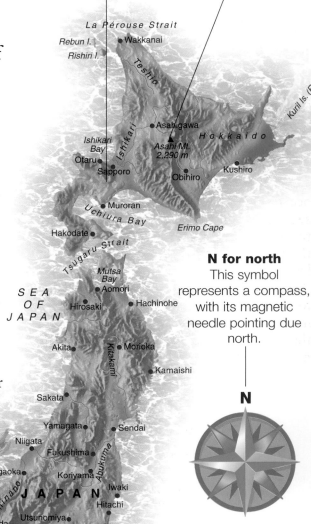

N for north

This symbol represents a compass, with its magnetic needle pointing due north.

Capital cities

The most important town in any country is called the capital city. This is very often the biggest town and is normally where the government makes the laws. Some capitals, however, are quite small.

Where in the world

If you want to find out where the regional map fits into a map of the whole world, check these small circular maps. The areas coloured in red show the location.

Key to symbols

■	Capitals
●	Towns
—	Rivers
—	Borders
	Lakes
	Mountains

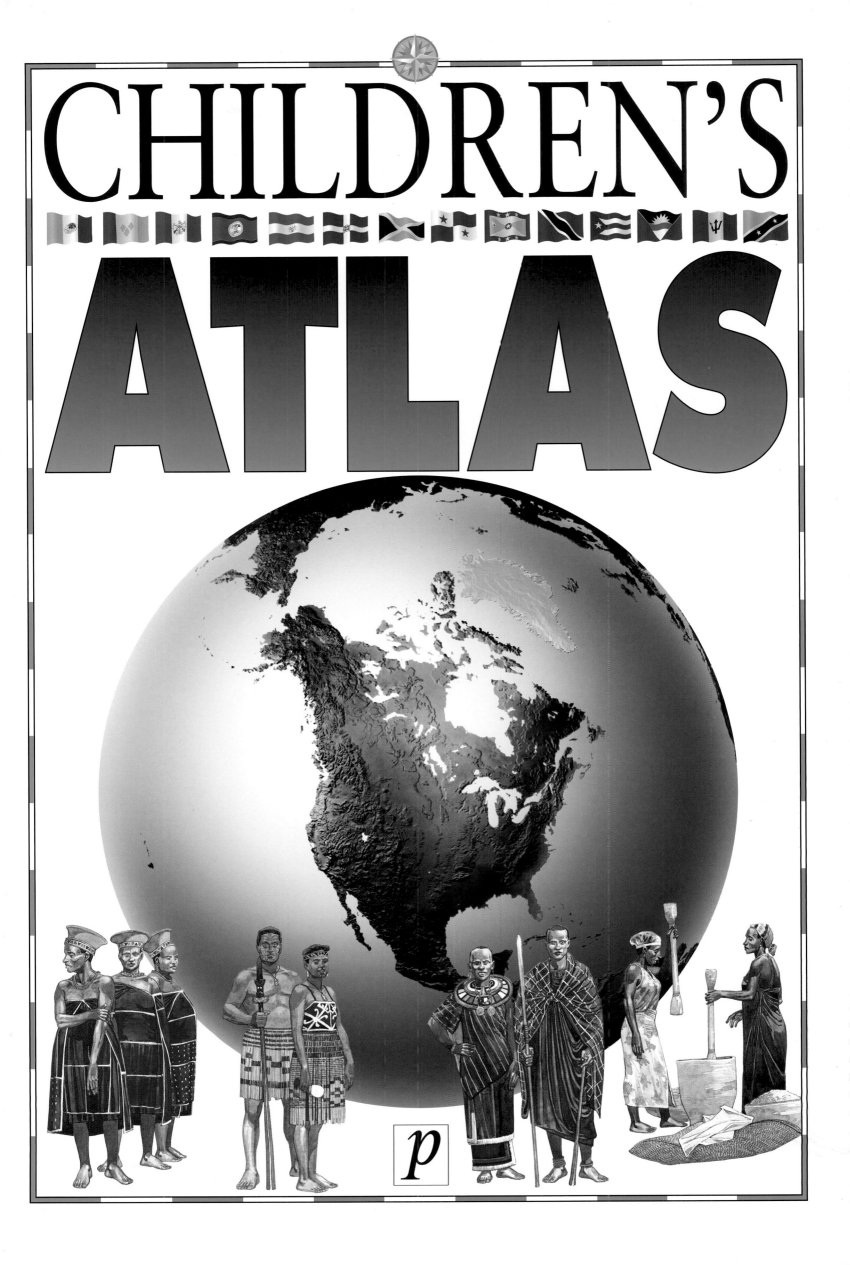

CHILDREN'S
ATLAS

p

This is a Parragon Book
This edition published in 2003

Parragon
Queen Street House
4 Queen Street
Bath BA1 1HE, UK

Copyright © Parragon 1998

British Library Cataloguing-in-Publication Data
A catalogue record for this book is available from the British Library

Printed in Indonesia

ISBN 1-40540-739-5

INTRODUCTION

EARTH FACTS

The world we live in is a huge ball of rock and metal spinning around, or rotating, in space. As the planet Earth rotates, it travels around the Sun, held on its path by a pulling force called gravity. The Earth is one of nine planets circling the Sun, and together they make up the Solar System.

When we see pictures of Earth taken from space, our planet appears blue, white and brown. The blue is the colour of the seas and oceans which cover over two-thirds of the Earth's surface. The swirling white patterns are the clouds – water vapour which hangs in the air, or atmosphere, surrounding the Earth's surface. The brown is the colour of the ground, which is divided into the Earth's landmasses or continents.

Photographs of the Earth's surface taken from space zoom in to show even more details – the world's great river systems, the high mountain ranges, the sprawling cities and the patchwork of crops that feed the hungry mouths of the world's population, which is now more than 6 billion.

PLANET EARTH
Circumference around the Equator: 40,075 kilometres
Circumference around the Poles: 40,008 kilometres
Diameter at the Equator: 12,756 kilometres
Surface area: About 510,000,000 square kilometres
Area covered by sea: 71 percent
Average distance from the Sun: 149,600,000 kilometres
Average distance from the Moon: 385,000 kilometres
Period of rotation: 23 hours 56 minutes
Speed of rotation: 1,660 kilometres per hour at the Equator
Period of revolution: 365 days 6 hours
Speed of revolution: 29.8 kilometres per second

FACT BOX

The world's highest peak
Mount Everest or Qomolangma, between Nepal and China, is the highest point on the Earth's surface.

HIGHEST PEAKS

Mountain	Height	Location
Everest (Qomolangma)	8,848 m	China-Nepal
K2 (Qogir Feng)	8,611 m	India-Pakistan
Kanchenjunga	8,586 m	India-Nepal
Makalu 1	8,463 m	China-Nepal
Dhaulagiri 1	8,167 m	Nepal
Nanga Parbat	8,125 m	India
Annapurna 1	8,091 m	Nepal
Gosainthan (Xixabangma Feng)	8,012 m	China
Distaghil Sar	7,885 m	India
Nanda Devi	7,816 m	India

LONGEST RIVERS

River	Length	Location
Nile	6,670 km	North Africa
Amazon	6,448 km	South America
Chang Jiang (Yangtze)	6,300 km	Central China
Mississippi-Missouri-Red	6,020 km	North America
Yenisey-Angara-Selenga	5,540 km	Mongolia-Russia
Huang He	5,464 km	Northern China
Ob-Irtysh	5,409 km	Russia-Kazakhstan
Zaïre (Congo)	4,700 km	Central Africa
Lena-Kirenga	4,400 km	Russia
Mekong	4,350 km	Southeast Asia

LARGEST LAKES

Lake	Area	Location
Caspian Sea	371,800 sq km	Central Asia
Superior	82,103 sq km	USA-Canada
Victoria	69,484 sq km	East Africa
Aral Sea	65,500 sq km	Central Asia
Huron	59,569 sq km	USA-Canada
Michigan	57,757 sq km	USA-Canada
Tanganyika	32,893 sq km	East Africa
Baikal	31,449 sq km	Russia
Great Bear	31,328 sq km	Canada
Malawi	28,878 sq km	Southern Africa

LARGEST ISLANDS

Island	Area
Greenland	2,1830 sq km
New Guinea	821,000 sq km
Borneo	727,900 sq km
Madagascar	589,081 sq km
Baffin	509,214 sq km
Sumatra	431,982 sq km
Honshu	228,204 sq km
Great Britain	218,800 sq km
Victoria	212,200 sq km
Ellesmere	196,917 sq km

MAJOR WATERFALLS
Highest Waterfalls

	Height	Location
Angel Falls	979 m	Venezuela
Mardsalsfossen	774 m	Norway
Yosemite	739 m	United States

Greatest volume

Waterfall	Volume	Location
Boyoma	17,000 cu m per sec	Dem. Rep. Congo (Zaïre)

OCEANS

Name	Area
Pacific	166,242,000 sq km
Atlantic	106,000,000 sq km
Indian	73,500,000 sq km
Arctic	14,350,000 sq km

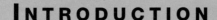

COUNTRIES OF THE WORLD

To the glory of God
Places of worship vary greatly around the world. This Christian cathedral, St Basil's, was built in the 1500s in Moscow, capital of today's Russian Federation.

There are about 192 countries in the world that are recognized as 'independent' nations, which means that they govern themselves. Many other lands are colonies or 'dependencies', which means that they are governed by other nations. The numbers change very often, as one country joins up with another one, or another splits up into separate nations. For example, the Indonesian province of East Timor became an independent nation in 2002.

Some countries are huge, some are tiny. The Russian Federation is the largest, with an area of 17,078,005 square kilometres. The smallest is Vatican City, at just 0.4 square kilometres. Some countries are home to just one people, while others are made up of many different peoples or ethnic groups, each with their own way of life and customs. Some people have no national borders of their own. For example the traditional homeland of the Kurdish people is divided between Turkey, Iraq and Iran.

The peoples of the world live very different lives. They have different faiths and beliefs, eat different foods and speak over 5000 different languages. Some people are very poor while others are very rich. However, the people on our planet also have many things in common. The spread of radio, television and other communications links in recent years has made the world a smaller place. Once it took years to travel around the world, but today we can get on a plane or keep in touch with each other at the push of a button.

Most of the world's countries are linked by agreements or treaties. Many European countries belong to the European Union, while African nations belong to the Organization of African Unity. Nearly all countries belong to the United Nations, which tries to prevent conflict and to build links between the world's nations.

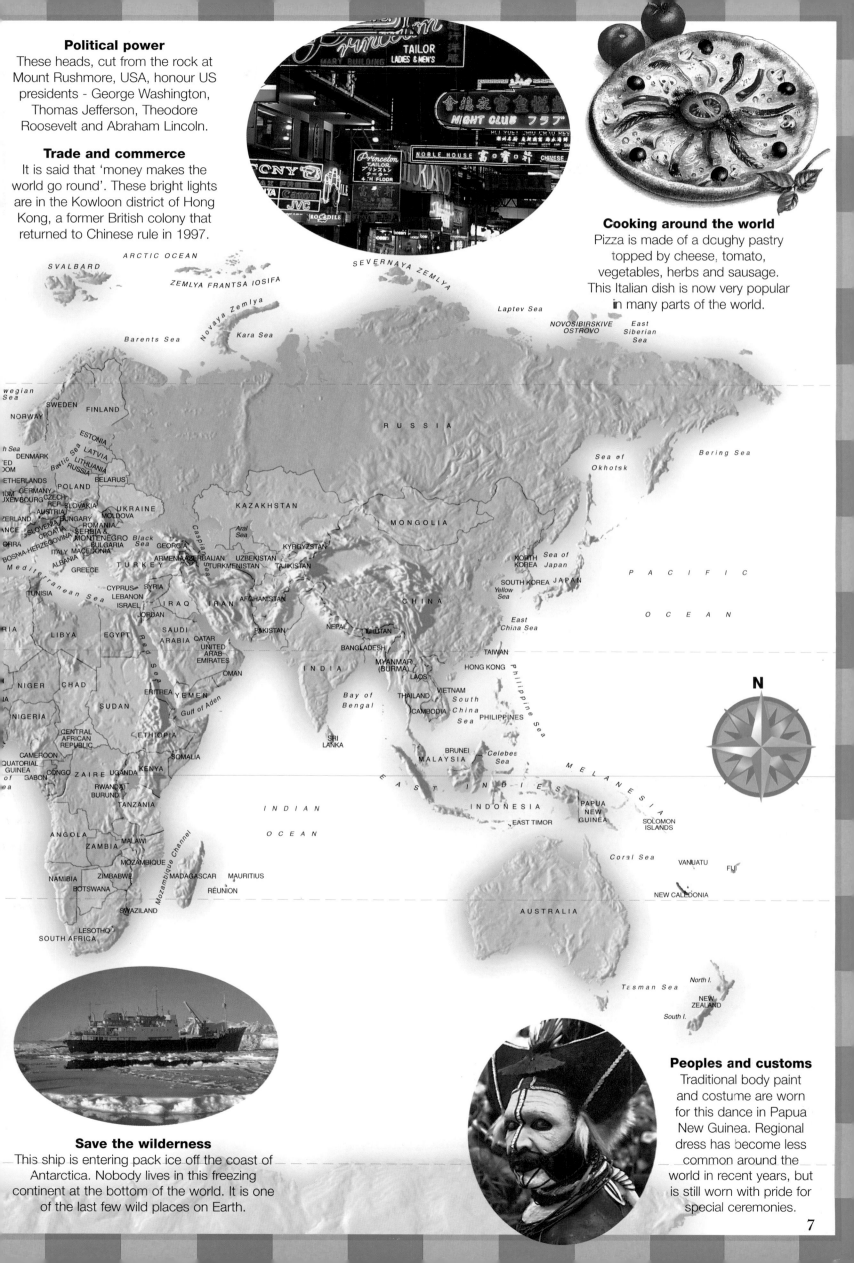

Political power
These heads, cut from the rock at Mount Rushmore, USA, honour US presidents - George Washington, Thomas Jefferson, Theodore Roosevelt and Abraham Lincoln.

Trade and commerce
It is said that 'money makes the world go round'. These bright lights are in the Kowloon district of Hong Kong, a former British colony that returned to Chinese rule in 1997.

Cooking around the world
Pizza is made of a doughy pastry topped by cheese, tomato, vegetables, herbs and sausage. This Italian dish is now very popular in many parts of the world.

Save the wilderness
This ship is entering pack ice off the coast of Antarctica. Nobody lives in this freezing continent at the bottom of the world. It is one of the last few wild places on Earth.

Peoples and customs
Traditional body paint and costume are worn for this dance in Papua New Guinea. Regional dress has become less common around the world in recent years, but is still worn with pride for special ceremonies.

SCANDINAVIA AND FINLAND

TWO PENINSULAS extend from northwestern Europe, shaped rather like the claws of a crab. The southern peninsula, extending from Germany, is called Jutland.

Together with a chain of islands which includes Fyn, Sjælland, and Lolland, Jutland makes up the nation of **Denmark**. Most of Denmark is flat and low-lying, a country of green farmland. It exports bacon and dairy products.

Across the windy channels of Sgagerrak and Kattegat, between the North and Baltic Seas, lies the long northern peninsula occupied by **Sweden** and **Norway**. This is a land shaped by movements of ice in prehistoric times. Glaciers carved out the deep sea inlets called fjords along its ragged western coast. Ranges of mountains run down the peninsula like a backbone. They descend to a land of forests, bogs and thousands of lakes.

Summers can be warm, but winters are bitterly cold, with heavy snow. Norway lives by fishing and its North Sea rigs make it Western Europe's largest producer of oil and natural gas. Sweden is a major exporter of timber, paper, wooden furniture and motor vehicles.

The three nations of Denmark, Sweden and Norway form the region of Scandinavia. It was from here that the seafarers known as Vikings set out about 1,200 years ago. The Vikings raided and settled the coasts of Western Europe, traded in Russia and the Middle East, settled Iceland and Greenland and even reached North America. Today's Danes, Swedes and Norwegians are all closely related, as are the Germanic languages that they speak.

The Arctic lands of northern Scandinavia are home to the Saami (or Lapps), a people who traditionally lived by herding reindeer. Their neighbours are the Finns and the Russians.

Finland is a land of lakes, with coasts on the Gulfs of Bothnia and Finland. Its forests make it a leading producer of wood pulp and paper. Helsinki is the capital.

RUSSIA

Vadsø
Kirkenes
Polmak
North Cape
Utsjoki
Inarijärvi
Sodankylä
Pelkosenniemi
Rovaniemi
Karasjok
Enontekiö
Hammerfest
Alta
Mt. Haltia 1,324m
Vittangi
Oulu
Kemi
Tornio
Luleå
Piteå
Boden
Gällivare
Tromsø
Kiruna
Mt. Kebnekaise 2,111m
Jokkmokk
Narvik
LOFOTEN VESTERÅLEN
Skellefte
Sorsele
Bodø
Störuman
Mosjøen

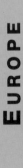

FINLAND

ICELAND

Grimsey
Raufarhöfn
Kópasker
Vopnafjördur
Seydisfjördur
Neskaupstadur
Búdir
Djúpivogur
Jökulsá á Fjöllum
Myvatn
Húsavik
Skálfandafljót
Akureyri
Eskifjördur
Höfn
VATNAJÖKULL
Hvannadalshnúkur 2,119m
Ólafsfjördur
Saudárkrókur
HOFSJÖKULL
Blanda
Porisvatn
Hekla 1,491 m
Ísafjördur
Thingeyri
Hólmavik
Blönduós
LANGJÖKULL
Hvitá
Pjórsá
Vik
Vatneyri
Breidafjördur
Stykkishólmur
Pingvallavatn
MYRDALSJÖKULL
Surtsey
Olafsvik
Borgarnes
Reykjavik
Stokkseyri
Heimaey
Akranes
Keflavik
Vestmannaeyjar

ICELAND

8

FINLAND

SWEDEN

NORWAY

DENMARK

NORWEGIAN SEA

Kattegat

Skagerrak

Baltic Sea

GERMANY

Stockholm, the heart of Sweden

The Swedish capital, Stockholm, is built between Lake Mälar and the Baltic Sea. The city covers several islands. It includes the mediaeval Old Town, merchants' houses from the 1900s and many modern factories and offices.

People of the Arctic

The Saami people live in Lapland, a region which extends right across the Scandinavian Arctic. Traditionally they are a nomadic people, who follow their herds of reindeer.

The Little Mermaid

This bronze statue in the Danish capital, Copenhagen, shows a character from one of the children's stories by Hans Christian Andersen (1805-75). Andersen created some of the world's best loved fairy tales.

NORWAY

SWEDEN

DENMARK

N

LOW COUNTRIES

THE COUNTRY OF THE NETHERLANDS is sometimes called Holland, but that is really the name of just two of its provinces, North and South Holland. This is a very flat, low-lying part of northern Europe. Long barriers and sea walls have been built to protect the countryside from North Sea floods. Large areas of land called polders have been reclaimed from the sea over the ages.

1600s by trading with Southeast Asia. Its capital city, Amsterdam, still has many beautiful old houses and canals dating back to this golden age. The Netherlands today remain a centre of commerce, exporting bulbs and cut flowers, vegetables and dairy products, especially cheese, and also electrical goods. Rotterdam is the world's busiest seaport. Peoples of the Netherlands include the Dutch and the Frisians, as well as people whose families came from former Dutch colonies in Indonesia and Surinam.

After a period under Spanish rule, the **Netherlands** became wealthy in the

The Flemish people of **Belgium** are closely related to the Dutch and their two languages are very similar. Belgium is also home to a French-speaking people, the Walloons, who mostly live in the south of the country. Much of the countryside in Belgium is also low and flat, but the land rises to the wooded hills of the Ardennes in the south. The country is heavily industrialized, and is also known for its fine foods – chocolates, pâtés, hams and traditional beers.

Luxembourg is a tiny country, a survivor of the age when most of Europe was divided into little states, principalities and duchies. However, modern industry and banking have made Luxembourg wealthy and successful. The people of Luxembourg speak French, German and a local language called Letzebuergesch.

The three countries have close ties. In 1948, after the terrible years of World War II (1939-45), Belgium, the Netherlands and Luxembourg set up an economic union called 'Benelux'. In 1957 they went on to what is now the European Union (EU).

Bruges skyline
The brick gables of old merchants' houses make a pleasing skyline in many historical towns of the Lowlands. Bruges has been famous through the ages for its lacemaking. The city is linked by canal to the seaport of Zeebrugge.

Wetlands butterfly
The Large Copper butterfly is on the endangered species list in both Belgium and the Netherlands. The butterfly thrives in flooded fields. Its caterpillar can survive underwater for many weeks. However draining of wetlands by farmers and roadbuilders threatens its survival.

NETHERLANDS

Enschede
Almelo
Emmen
Assen
Groningen
Meppel
Zwolle
Apeldoorn
IJssel
Leeuwarden
Sneek
North-East Polder
Flevoland Polder
Markerwaard Polder (planned)
Barrier Dam
IJsselmeer
Ameland
Terscheling
West Frisian Islands
Vlieland
Texel
Waddenzee
Hilversum
Amsterdam
Zaanstad
Haarlem
Alkmaar

'When it's spring again...'

The classic Dutch landscape includes fields of brilliantly coloured tulips and old-fashioned windmills. Both attract the tourists and are seen here near the town of Haarlem.

Dutch cheese

Another popular attraction in the Netherlands is the cheese market at Alkmaar. The Netherlands exports mild cheeses such as Edam and Gouda around the world.

GERMANY

GERMANY

LUXEMBOURG

Arnhem

Venlo

Nijmegen

Maas

s'Hertogenbosch

Eindhoven

Waal

Lek

Tilburg

Breda

Heerlen

Maastricht

Vaalserberg 321m

Verviers

▲ *Botrange 694m*

Spa

▲ *Buurgplatz 559m*

Luxembourg

Esch-sur-Alzette

Genk

Hasselt

Liège

Meuse

ARDENNES MOUNTAINS

Bastogne

Libramont

LUXEMBOURG

Rotterdam

Dordrecht

he Hague

Delft

Huy

Leuven (Louvain)

Mechelen

Waterloo

Antwerp

St. Niklaas

Sambre Namur

Dinant

BELGIUM

Charleroi

La Louvière

Brussels

Aalst

Mons

NETHERLANDS

Oosterschelde

Vlissingen

Westerschelde

Zeebrugge

Bruges

Ostend

Roeslare

Kortijk

Ghent

Schelde

Tournai

BELGIUM

FRANCE

N

The future – 1958 style

This strange looking landmark is the Atomium. It was built for the World Fair held in Brussels in 1958 and was meant to be a symbol of a new age of atomic science and technology.

BRITISH ISLES

THE BRITISH ISLES lie off the northwestern coast of Europe, between the shallow waters of the North Sea and the stormy Atlantic Ocean. Their western shores are warmed by an ocean current called the North Atlantic Drift. The climate is mild, with a high rainfall in the west.

The largest island is called **Great Britain**, and its three countries (**England**, **Scotland** and **Wales**) are joined together within a United Kingdom. The second largest of the British Isles is called **Ireland**. Most of Ireland is an independent republic, but part of the north is governed as a province of the United Kingdom.

Great Britain has a landscape of rolling farmland. There are rugged highlands in Wales and Scotland, while England has rich farmland in the southeast, bleak moors in the north, flat fields in East Anglia and wild coasts in Cornwall. There are many beautiful old villages and towns, but also large cities and ports.

The Irish landscape is less crowded. It has green fields, misty hills and, in the west, steep cliffs pounded by Atlantic breakers. Its capital, Dublin, lies on the River Liffey.

English is spoken throughout the British Isles, but other languages may be heard too – Welsh, Irish and Scots Gaelic, and the various languages spoken by British people of Asian and African descent.

Both the UK and the **Republic of Ireland** are members of the European Union.

FACT BOX

◆ **United Kingdom:**
England, Scotland, Wales,
N. Ireland
Area: 242,480 sq km
Population: 58,789,000
Capital: London
Official language: English
Currency: Sterling pound

◆ **England**
Area: 130,420 sq km
Population: 49,139,000
Capital: London
Official language: English
Currency: Sterling pound

◆ **Scotland**
Area: 77,170 sq km
Population: 5,062,000
Capital: Edinburgh
Official language: English
Currency: Sterling pound

◆ **Wales**
Area: 20,770 sq km
Population: 2,903,000
Capital: Cardiff
Official language: Welsh, English
Currency: Sterling pound

◆ **Northern Ireland**
Area: 14,150 sq km
Population: 1,685,000
Capital: Belfast
Official language: English
Currency: Sterling pound

◆ **Republic of Ireland**
Area: 70,283 sq km
Population: 3,823,000
Capital: Dublin
Official language: English, Irish
Currency: Euro

Highland games
Scottish pipers parade in the Highland Games. This competition has been taking place since the early nineteenth century, but has its roots

Wren
One of the most widespread birds of Britain, this short drab coloured bird with a cocked tail, has a loud warbling song. Wrens feed on caterpillars, beetles and bugs.

NORTH SEA

SHETLAND ISLANDS
Unst
Yell
Foula
Sumburgh Head
Lerwick
Fair Isle

Westray
Kirkwall
Hoy
South Ronaldsay
ORKNEY ISLANDS
John o'Groats
Thurso

Cape Wrath

SCOTLAND

Fraserburgh
Peterhead
Aberdeen
Dee
Don
Spey
Inverness
Moray Firth
Loch Ness
NORTH WEST HIGHLANDS
GRAMPIAN MTS.
Ben Nevis ▲ 1,343 m
Mallaig
Oban

Montrose
SIDLAW HILLS
Dundee
Tay
Firth of Forth
OCHIL HILLS
Perth
Loch Lomond
Forth
Edinburgh
St. Abbs Head
Berwick-upon-Tweed
Holy I.
Glasgow
Greenock
Clyde
Tweed
Jedburgh
UPLANDS
HILLS

Butt of Lewis
Stornoway
North Minch
Lewis
OUTER HEBRIDES
North Uist
South Uist
Barra
Skye
Rhum
Coll
Tiree
Mull
Jura
Islay
Kintyre Pen.
Arran
Ayr
Kilmarnock
INNER HEBRIDES
NORTHERN IRELAND
Malin Head
Tory I.
Rathlin I.

12

UNITED KINGDOM

ENGLAND

UNITED KINGDOM

REPUBLIC OF IRELAND

Tower of London

Built in the eleventh century by William the Conqueror, this ancient fortress on the river Thames was once a royal home. It is now a museum and houses the crown jewels. It was here that Anne Boleyn, wife of Henry VIII, was beheaded. Yeomen of the Guard, or Beefeaters, still guard the Tower.

Ladies' View, Killarney, Eire

This famous beauty spot in southern Ireland enjoys wonderful views of Macgillycuddyís Reeks (a mountain range) and the lakes of Killarney. Of these lakes Lough Learne, or lower lake, is the largest with over 30 islands.

ENGLAND

Norwich
Flamborough Head
Spurn Head
Kingston upon Hull
Scarborough
Middlesbrough
Durham
NORTH YORK MOORS
Swale
York
Leeds
Bradford
Oldham
Sheffield
Rotherham
Manchester
Preston
Blackpool
Wigan
Liverpool
Llandudno
Stoke on Trent
Wrexham
Derby
Nottingham
Leicester
Wolverhampton
Walsall
Birmingham
Coventry
Northampton
Milton Keynes
Peterborough EAST ANGLIA
Cambridge
Ipswich
Colchester
Chelmsford
Luton
London
Thames
Reading
Oxford
Swindon
Basingstoke
Salisbury
Winchester
Southampton
Portsmouth
Bournemouth
Southend-on-Sea
Canterbury
Dover
Folkestone
Hastings
Brighton
Isle of Wight

LINCOLN WOLDS
THE FENS
The Wash
Welland
Trent
CHILTERNS
NORTH DOWNS
THE WEALD
SOUTH DOWNS
HAMPSHIRE DOWNS
COTSWOLD HILLS
Severn
Wye
Cheltenham
Gloucester
Bristol
Newport
Cardiff
Swansea
MENDIP HILLS
EXMOOR
Bridgwater
Ilfracombe
Bristol Channel
Exeter
Torbay
DARTMOOR
Plymouth
Portland Bill
Lyme Bay
Bude
Lundy
St. Ives
Penzance
Lands End
Lizard Point
ISLES OF SCILLY
Alderney
CHANNEL ISLANDS
Guernsey
Jersey
ENGLISH CHANNEL

Carlisle
Lake District
Scafell Pike 978 m
Walney I.
Morecambe Bay
Isle of Man
Douglas
IRISH SEA
Anglesey
Holyhead
Caernarfon
Snowdon 1,085 m
Cardigan Bay
Aberystwyth
Cardigan
Carmarthen
Milford Haven
Gower Peninsula
St. Brides Bay
Bardsey I.

WALES
CAMBRIAN MTS.
WALES

Stranraer
Solway Firth
CHANNEL

NORTHERN IRELAND
ANTRIM MTS.
Belfast
Lough Neagh
Armagh
Slieve Donard 862 m
Dundalk
Boyne
Dublin
Dun Laoghaire
WICKLOW MTS.
Wicklow Head
Wexford
Hook Head

IRELAND
SPERRIN MTS.
Donegal
Donegal Bay
Sligo
Lough Allen
Lower Lough Erne
Upper Lough Erne
Lough Ree
Athlone
Lough Derg
BOG OF ALLEN
Liffey
Barrow
Carlow
Nore
Waterford
GALTY MTS.
Blackwater
Tipperary
Cork
Old Head of Kinsale
Shannon
Limerick
Lough Corrib
Lough Mask
Galway
Galway Bay
ARAN ISLANDS
Loop Head
Dingle Bay
Gt. Blasket I.
Kenmare River
Bantry Bay
Bantry
Killarney
Carrauntoohill 1,041 m
Mizen Head

OCEAN
Erris Head
Achill Head
Clew Bay
Lough Conn

13

FRANCE AND MONACO

Château de Charumont
France has many historical castles, palaces and stately homes, or châteaux. Some of the finest are in the Loire valley.

FRANCE IS A LARGE, beautiful country which lies at the heart of Western Europe. Its western regions include the massive peaks of the Pyrenees, vineyards and pine forests, peaceful rivers and Atlantic shores.

The north includes the stormy headlands of Brittany, the cliffs of Normandy and the Channel ports. Rolling fertile plains are drained by the winding river Seine, over whose banks and islands sprawls the French capital. Paris is one of the world's great cities, with broad avenues, historic palaces and churches.

The west of **France** is bordered by wooded hills which rise to the high forested slopes of the Jura mountains and finally the spectacular glaciers and ridges of the Alps. The rocks of the Massif Central, shaped by ancient volcanoes, rise in central southern France, to the west of the Rhône valley. The sun-baked hills of southern France border the warm seas of the Mediterranean Sea. This coast includes the wetlands of the Camargue, the great seaport of Marseilles and the fashionable yachting marinas of Cannes.

France has played a major part in history, and the French language is now spoken in many parts of the world. The French people are mostly descended from a Celtic people called the Gauls and Germanic peoples, such as the Franks and Vikings. Within France are several other peoples with their own languages and distinct cultures, such as Bretons, Basques, Catalans, Alsatians, Corsicans and Algerians.

France is a republic belonging to the European Union (EU) and is an important industrial power, producing cars, aerospace equipment, chemicals and textiles. The country is renowned for its wines, its cheeses, and its fine cooking.

Part of the Mediterranean coast is occupied by a very small principality called **Monaco**. It has close links with its large neighbour and shares the same currency. The state is famous for its casino.

Cape Corse

Bastia

CORSICA

Gulf of Sagone

Ajaccio

Bonifacio

Strait of Bonifacio

Cherbour
Carenta
S
Gulf of St-Malo Gran
Morlaix St.-Malo
Brest St-Brieuc Dinan
Fouge
Douernenez Pontivy
Quimper Rennes
Lorient
Vannes
Redon
St. Nazaire
Belle-Ile
Nantes
La Roche-sur-Y
Isle d'Yeu
Les Sables-d'Olor
Ré I.
La Roche
Roche
Oléron
Roy
Pau

Sacré-Coeur
The gleaming domes of this church soar above the Parisian district of Montmartre, once famed as the haunt of artists and writers.

Bayonn
Biarritz

S P A I

Shape of the future
The Futuroscope theme park and study centre, near Poitiers, is one example of France's many experimental modern buildings. This theatre looks like a huge crystal.

Vineyard harvest
Grapes are gathered at a vineyard in Alsace, on the slopes of the Vosges. Grapes, grown in many regions of France, are made into some of the world's finest wines.

Quiche Lorraine
A speciality of north-eastern France, this is a baked pastry tart filled with eggs, cream, cheese and bacon.

FACT BOX

◆ **Germany**
Area: 356,840sq km
Population: 82,300,000
Capital: Berlin
Official language: German
Currency: Euro

GERMANY

NORTH SEA

BALTIC SEA

Sylt

Flensburg

Schleswig

Kiel Bay

Fehmarn

Rügen

Helgoland

Kiel

Rendsburg

Mecklenburg Bay

Stralsund

Neumünster

Rostock

Cuxhaven

Itzehoe

Lübeck

Wismar

Güstrow

Neubrandenburg

Elmshorn

Norderstedt

Schwerin

Wilhelmshaven

Bremerhaven

Hamburg

Emden

Buxtehude

Müritz Lake

Neustrelitz

Papenburg

Oldenburg

Bremen

Lüneburg

Delmenhorst

Weser

Wittenberge

Eberswalde-Finow

NETHERLANDS

Ems

Vechta

Nienburg

Celle

Uelzen

Elbe

Stendal

Oder

Nordhorn

Rheine

Weser

Hannover

Aller

Wolfsburg

Brandenburg

Berlin

Osnabrück

Minden

Hildesheim

Brunswick (Braunschweig)

Potsdam

Frankfurt (an der Oder)

Gronau

TEUTOBURG FOREST

Bielefeld

Hameln

Salzgitter

Magdeburg

Münster

Holzminden

Bad Harzburg

Halberstadt

Dessau

Eisenhüttenstadt

Rhine

Bocholt

Hamm

Paderborn

Leine

HARZ MTS.

Elbe

Cottbus

Dinslaken

Göttingen

Halle

Hoyerswerda

Duisburg

Dortmund

Arnsberg

Kassel

Münden

Nordhausen

Leipzig

Neisse

Krefeld

Essen

Meissen

Mönchen-Gladbach

Wuppertal

GERMANY

Mühlhausen

Weimar

Gör

Düsseldorf

Remscheid

Solingen

Marburg

Erfurt

Jena

Gera

Dresden

Cologne (Köln)

Bergisch-Gladbach

Chemnitz

Freiberg

Aachen

Bonn

Siegen

Alsfeld

THURINGIAN FOREST

Zwickau

BELGIUM

Neuwied

Giessen

Fulda

Fulda

Werra

Suhl

Plauen

Koblenz

Main

Hof

LUXEMBOURG

Daun

Rhine

Wiesbaden

Frankfurt am Main

Coburg

CZECH REPUBLIC

Trier

Mosel

Mainz

Offenbach

Schweinfurt

Bayreuth

HUNSRÜCK

Darmstadt

Main

Würzburg

STEIGERWALD

Bamberg

BOHEMIAN FOREST

Saar

Worms

Kitzingen

Ludwigshafen

Mannheim

Kaiserslautern

Jagst

Fürth

Nuremberg (Nürnberg)

Saarbrücken

Heidelberg

Karlsruhe

Heilbronn

Regensburg

Pforzheim

FRANCE

Baden-Baden

Stuttgart

Aalen

Ingolstadt

Passau

Neckar

Tübingen

SWABIAN JURA

Danube

N

Reutlingen

Ulm

Augsburg

Inn

Braunau

Rhine

BLACK FOREST

Munich (München)

Rosenheim

Salzach

Freiburg

Memmingen

Lech

Konstanz

Kempten

Lake Constance (Bodensee)

Zugspitze 2,963 m

Kufstein

SWITZERLAND

LIECHTENSTEIN

AUSTRIA

GERMANY

GERMANY IS ONE OF EUROPE'S most populated countries. Lying at the heart of Europe, its varied landscapes reflect western, central and eastern Europe.

The rolling hills and heathland of central Germany stretch to the North Sea. In the west the rivers Rhine and Moselle wind through steep valleys planted with vines, where world-famous white wines are produced. In the northeast a vast plain of rolling farmland and wooded hills is bordered by the Baltic Sea and by the rivers Oder and Neisse. In the northwest are sandy heathlands and marshy peatlands. To the south, the landscape becomes more dramatic as mountainous Bavaria rises to meet the Alps along the Austrian border. Here, the jagged peaks and Alpine scenery attract tourists and hikers.

About a third of the country is still wooded, with much of the uplands covered in forest. The Black Forest in the southwest is so-named because of its dark fir trees.

In southern Germany, winters are cold and snowfall is frequent. Summers are generally warm with plenty of sunshine.

For most of its history Germany has been divided into different states. Today's united Germany dates from 1990. Germany is a federal republic, which means that its regions or Länder have considerable powers. The country is a leading member of the European Union and is a major world producer of cars, electrical and household goods, medicines, chemicals, wines and beers.

German is spoken throughout the country with a great variety of dialects.

The Volkswagen
The world-famous Volkswagen, or "people's car", is produced in Germany and has been popular in Europe since the 1960s. As well as Volkswagen, other successful German car companies include Mercedes and BMW.

Brimming with beer
Munich, capital of Bavaria in southern Germany, hosts a famous beer festival every October. Regional dress is still common in the region.

Vineyards
The Romans were the first people to plant vines in Germany. Today the chief vine-growing areas are in the southwest and along the Rhine and Moselle river valleys, where wine is made.

Medieval revelry
Festival costumes recall the Middle Ages in Baden Württemberg. During that period Germany was made up of many small states.

Good companion
The German Shepherd dog is brave, loyal, and responds very well to training. This makes it ideal for police work. Originally from Germany, it is now found worldwide.

IBERIAN PENINSULA

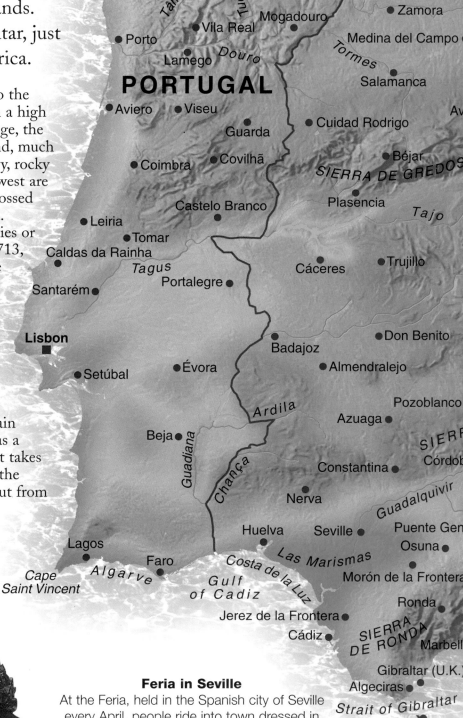

N

Bay of Biscay

THE IBERIAN PENINSULA is in southwestern Europe, and juts out into the Atlantic Ocean. It is bordered to the north by the stormy Bay of Biscay and to the south by the Mediterranean Sea and the Balearic Islands. Across the Strait of Gibraltar, just 13 kilometres away, lies the continent of Africa.

The north coast, green from high rainfall, rises to the Cantabrian mountains, while the snowy Pyrenees form a high barrier along the Spanish-French frontier. Another range, the Sierra Nevada, runs parallel with the south coast. Inland, much of the Iberian peninsula is taken up by an extremely dry, rocky plateau, which swelters in the heat of summer. To the west are forested highlands and the fertile plains of Portugal, crossed by great rivers such as the Douro, Tagus and Guadiana.

The Iberian peninsula is occupied by four countries or territories. There is **Gibraltar**, a British colony since 1713, and the tiny independent state of **Andorra**, high in the Pyrenees. The two main countries of the region are **Spain** and **Portugal**. Both have a history of overseas settlement, and both Spanish and Portuguese have become the chief languages of Latin America. Many people speak other languages, including Basque and Catalan, and have their own traditions and history.

Both Spain and Portugal were ruled by dictators for much of the 20th century, but today both are democracies and members of the European Union. Spain produces olives, citrus fruits, wines and sherries, and has a large fishing fleet. Portugal also produces wine and port takes its name from the city of Oporto. Fishing villages line the coasts and cork, used for bottle stoppers and tiling, is cut from the thick bark of the cork oak tree.

PORTUGAL

Feria in Seville
At the Feria, held in the Spanish city of Seville every April, people ride into town dressed in traditional finery. The river is lined with tents and pavilions. The festival is celebrated with bullfights, flamenco music and dancing.

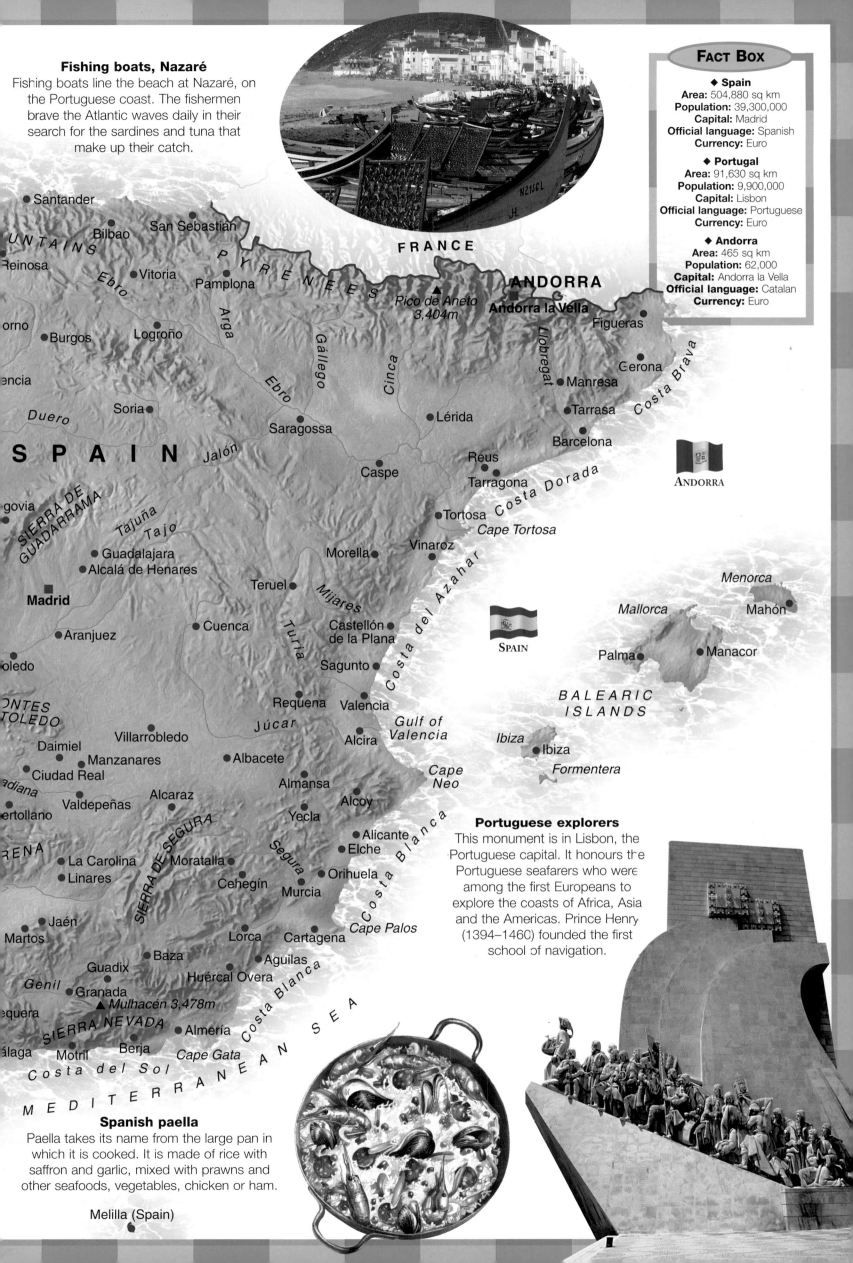

Fishing boats, Nazaré
Fishing boats line the beach at Nazaré, on the Portuguese coast. The fishermen brave the Atlantic waves daily in their search for the sardines and tuna that make up their catch.

FACT BOX

◆ **Spain**
Area: 504,880 sq km
Population: 39,300,000
Capital: Madrid
Official language: Spanish
Currency: Euro

◆ **Portugal**
Area: 91,630 sq km
Population: 9,900,000
Capital: Lisbon
Official language: Portuguese
Currency: Euro

◆ **Andorra**
Area: 465 sq km
Population: 62,000
Capital: Andorra la Vella
Official language: Catalan
Currency: Euro

FRANCE

ANDORRA

Santander

Bilbao
San Sebastian

MOUNTAINS

Reinosa
Vitoria
Pamplona

PYRENEES

Pico de Aneto
3,404m

Andorra la Vella

Figueras

orno

Burgos
Logroño

Ebro

Arga

Gállego

Ebro

Cinca

Llobregat

Gerona

Costa Brava

Manresa

encia

Soria

Duero

Saragossa

Lérida

Tarrasa

Barcelona

S P A I N

Jalón

Reus

Tarragona

Costa Dorada

govia

SIERRA DE GUADARRAMA

Tajuña

Tajo

Tortosa
Cape Tortosa

Vinaroz

Costa del Azahar

ANDORRA

Guadalajara
Alcalá de Henares

Morella

Madrid

Teruel

Mijares

Menorca

Mallorca

Mahón

Aranjuez

Cuenca

Castellón
de la Plana

SPAIN

Palma

Manacor

oledo

Turia

Sagunto

ONTES
TOLEDO

Requena
Valencia

Júcar

Alcira

Gulf of
Valencia

*BALEARIC
ISLANDS*

Villarrobledo

Albacete

Ibiza

Ibiza

Daimiel
Manzanares

Almansa

Cape
Neo

Formentera

Ciudad Real

Alcaraz

Alcoy

adiana

Valdepeñas

Yecla

ertollano

Costa Blanca

RENA

SIERRA DE SEGURA

Alicante

Elche

Portuguese explorers

La Carolina
Moratalla

Segura

Orihuela

This monument is in Lisbon, the Portuguese capital. It honours the Portuguese seafarers who were among the first Europeans to explore the coasts of Africa, Asia and the Americas. Prince Henry (1394–1460) founded the first school of navigation.

Linares

Cehegín

Murcia

Jaén

Cape Palos

Martos

Lorca
Cartagena

Baza
Aguilas

Guadix
Huércal Overa

Costa Blanca

Genil

Granada

Mulhacén 3,478m

equera

SIERRA NEVADA

Almería

MEDITERRANEAN SEA

álaga
Motril
Berja

Cape Gata

Costa del Sol

Spanish paella
Paella takes its name from the large pan in which it is cooked. It is made of rice with saffron and garlic, mixed with prawns and other seafoods, vegetables, chicken or ham.

Melilla (Spain)

ITALY AND THE ALPS

THE SNOWY PEAKS of the Alps form the highest mountain chain in western Europe. They run in a wide arc through Switzerland and Austria. Stretching southwards, Italy occupies a long, boot-shaped peninsula that extends into the Mediterranean Sea.

Switzerland's beautiful landscape and historical towns attract many tourists. Industries include dairy produce, precision instruments and finance. Zurich is a world centre of banking, while Geneva is the headquarters of the Red Cross and the World Health Organization. To the east, the tiny country of **Liechtenstein** is closely linked with Switzerland and uses the same currency. The land of **Italy**, **Austria** descends from the soaring peaks of the Alps to the flat Danube river valley. Austria's main industries are tourism, farming, forestry and manufacture.

A long chain of mountains, the Appenines, runs down the spine of **Italy**, descending to coastal farmland and the hot, dry plains of the south. Olives and grapes grow well in the sunny climate, and Italy is the largest wine producer in the world. Factories produce cars, textiles and leather goods.

In ancient times Rome was the capital of a vast empire that stretched across western Europe, southwest Asia and North Africa. During the 1400s and 1500s Italy saw a great flowering of scholarship and the arts, known as the Renaissance. Italian, based on the ancient Latin language,

River of ice

This impressive glacier grinds its way down the Alps near Zermatt. Many tourists and climbers visit Switzerland to enjoy the spectacular views and to ski.

AUSTRIA

SWITZERLAND

LIECHTENSTEIN

CZECH REPUBLIC

HUNGARY

AUSTRIA

Passau
Braunau
Linz
Krems
St Pölten
Baden
Vienna
Bruck
Neusiedler See
Wels
Gmunden
Steyr
Wiener Neustadt
Kapfenberg
Leoben
Graz
Wolfsberg
Salzburg
Hallein
Salzach
Enns
Mur
Klagenfurt
Villach
Drava
HOHE TAUERN
NIEDERE TAUERN
Grossglockner 2,863 m
SLOVENIA
Kufstein
Kitzbühel
Innsbruck
Inn
Brenner
Bolzano
Trento
Trieste
Udine
Portogruaro
Venice
Piave
Borgo
Treviso
Chioggia
Vicenza
Padua
Adria
Verona
L. Garda
Comacchio
Ravenna
Rimini
San Marino
SAN MARINO
Pesaro
Ancona
Iesi
Macerata
Gubbio
Cortona
Arezzo
Forli
Bologna
Po
Reno
Panaro
Ferrara
Carpi
Modena
Reggio nell'Emilia
Mantova
Oglio
Brescia
Bergamo
Lecco
Monza
Lodi
Cremona
Pavia
Milan
Piacenza
Parma
A
Pistoia
Lucca
Florence
Arno
Siena
Livorno
Pisa
Viareggio
Massa
Carrara
La Spezia
LIGURIAN SEA
Gulf of Genoa
Genoa
Savona
Novi Ligure
Alessandra
Biella
Cuneo
Turin
Tanaro
MONACO
FRANCE

GERMANY
LIECHTENSTEIN
Vaduz
Schaffhausen
Konstanz
Lake Constance (Bodensee)
Winterthur
St Gallen
Zurich
Baden
Zug
Lucerne
Chur
Davos
St Moritz
LEPONTINE ALPS
Bellinzona
Locarno
Lugano
L. Maggiore
Como
L. Como
Ticino
Andermatt
SWITZERLAND
Interlaken
BERNESE ALPS
Bern
Thun
Zermatt
Monte Rosa ▲ 4,634m
Matterhorn ▲ 4,478 m
Mont Blanc 4,807m
Martigny
Montreux
Thonon
Geneva
Lake Geneva
Lausanne
Fribourg
Lake Neuchâtel
Neuchâtel
Solothurn
Basel
Zugspitze 2,963 m
R
SWITZERLAND

20

Surrounded by Italian territory are two small independent states. One is **Vatican City**, the world's smallest country. It is a district of Rome and headquarters for the Pope and the Roman Catholic Church. The other is tiny **San Marino**.

South of Italy is **Malta**. The Maltese have their own language and live from building and repairing ships and from tourism.

The Leaning Tower

This famous bell tower was built in the Italian city of Pisa during the Middle Ages, on unstable ground, and it soon began to sink. Today it leans from the vertical by about 5 metres.

Venice carnival

Elegant masks, cloaks and costumes in the style of the 1700s disguise revellers at Venice's famous carnival. Venice is one of the most beautiful cities in Europe.

On the Gulf of Salerno

The Italian seaport of Amalfi lies at the foot of Monte Cerreto, to the southeast of the city of Naples. The scenery here is spectacular.

FACT BOX

◆ **Switzerland**
Area: 41,285 sq km
Population: 7,100,000
Capital: Bern
Official languages: German, French, Italian, Romansh
Currency: Swiss franc

◆ **Liechtenstein**
Area: 160 sq km
Population: 30,000
Capital: Vaduz
Official language: German
Currency: Euro

◆ **Austria**
Area: 83,855 sq km
Population: 8,100,000
Capital: Vienna
Official language: German
Currency: Euro

◆ **Italy**
Area: 301,245 sq km
Population: 57,100,000
Capital: Rome
Official language: Italian
Currency: Euro

◆ **Vatican City**
Area: 0.44 sq km
Population: 1,000
Official language: Latin
Currency: Euro

◆ **San Marino**
Area: 61 sq km
Population: 23,000
Capital: San Marino
Official language: Italian
Currency: Euro

◆ **Malta**
Area: 316 sq km
Population: 359,000
Capital: Valletta
Official languages: Maltese, English
Currency: Maltese lira

Map labels:

I T A L Y
Corno Grande 2,912m
Civitavecchia
Vatican City (in Rome)
Rome
Pescara
Vasto
Avezzano
Latina
Termoli
Agnone
Isernia
Benevento
▲Vesuvius 1,227m
Salerno
Naples
Gulf of Gaeta
Ischia
Capri
Gulf of Naples
L. Varano
Foggia
Melfi
Potenza
Altamura
Bari
Brindisi
Taranto
Lecce
Gallipoli
Gulf of Taranto
Tricase
Otranto
Belvedere Marittimo
Rossano
Cosenza
Catanzaro
Crotone
Vibo Valentia
Reggio di Calabria
Stromboli
Salina
Lipari
Vulcano
LIPARI ISLANDS
Messina
Mt Etna 3,340m
Catania
Gulf of Catania
S i c i l y
Palermo
Cape San Vito
Trapani
Alcamo
Mazara del Vallo
Caltanissetta
Agrigento
Gulf of Gela
Syracuse
Ragusa
M A L T A   C H A N N E L
Pantelleria
MALTA
MALTA

SAN MARINO
San Marino

VATICAN CITY

ITALY

Corsica (France)
Strait of Bonifacio
Gulf of Asinara
Asinara
Gulf of Orosei
Olbia
Sassari
Alghero
Nuoro
S a r d i n i a
Tirso
Oristano
Cagliari
Gulf of Cagliari
San Pietro
Giglio

CENTRAL EUROPE

THREE SMALL COUNTRIES cluster around the eastern shores of the Baltic Sea. **Estonia**, **Latvia** and **Lithuania** were part of the Soviet Union (today's Russian Federation) from 1940 until 1991, when they became independent. Their lands include forests and lakes, farmland and industrial cities.

Poland, which has historic links with Lithuania, is a large country which has also known invasions and foreign rule through much of its history. Despite this, the Poles, a Slavic people, have kept a sense of independence and a pride in their traditions. The lands near Poland's Baltic coast are dotted with lakes. The north is a flat land of pine forests, part of the great plain which stretches from eastern Germany into Russia. It is cold and snowy in winter, but warm in summer. In southern Poland the land rises to highlands and the jagged peaks of the Tatra mountains, along the Slovakian border.

Slovakia and the **Czech Republic** were a single country until 1993. Slovakia is a land of high mountains dropping to fertile farmland around the River Danube, which forms its southeastern border. When the two countries divided, most industry lay on the Czech side of the border. The Czech Republic produces beer, glass, ceramics, steel and machinery. The country is bordered by mountains and, in the east, by the Bohemian centre of learning and the arts.

The Czechs and Slovaks are both Slavic peoples, but the Hungarians are Magyars, a people who invaded and settled in the region about 1200 years ago. **Hungary** is a country of wide open plains and low mountains. Its fertile farmland produces fruits, grains and grapes for making strong red wine. Its beautiful capital, Budapest, is on the River Danube.

Historical Prague

Prague, capital of the Czech Republic, is a fine old city on the River Vltava. Prague was the chief city of independent Bohemia in the Middle Ages.

ESTONIA

LATVIA

LITHUANIA

RUSSIA

Lake Peipus

Kohtla-Järve

Tartu

Munamagi 318 m

Gaizina 311 m

Daugavpils

Utena

Ukmerge

Vilnius

311 m

E S T O N I A

L A T V I A

L I T H U A N I A

Parnu

Panevezys

Kaunas

Tallinn

Riga

Siauliai

Gulf of Riga

Jurmala

Jelgava

Saldus

Nemunas (Neman)

Ventspils

Liepāja

Klaipeda

Hiumaa

Saaremaa

POLAND

Kaliningrad (RUSSIA)

Gulf of Gdansk

N

FACT BOX

◆ **Poland**
 Area: 312,685 sq km
 Population: 38,600,000.
  Capital: Warsaw
 Official language: Polish
  Currency: Zloty

◆ **Czech Republic**
 Area: 78,864 sq km
 Population: 10,330,000
  Capital: Prague
 Official language: Czech
  Currency: Koruna

◆ **Slovakia**
 Area: 49,035 sq km
 Population: 5,400,000
  Capital: Bratislava
 Official language: Slovak
  Currency: Koruna

◆ **Hungary**
 Area: 93,034 sq km
 Population: 10,294,000
  Capital: Budapest
 Official language: Hungarian
  Currency: Forint

◆ **Latvia**
 Area: 63,700 sq km
 Population: 2,700,000
  Capital: Riga
 Official language: Latvian
  Currency: Lats

◆ **Lithuania**
 Area: 65,200 sq km
 Population: 3,742,000
  Capital: Kiev
 Official language: Vilnius
  Currency: Litas

◆ **Estonia**
 Area: 45,100 sq km
 Population: 1,517,000
  Capital: Tallinn
 Official language: Estonian
  Currency: Kroon

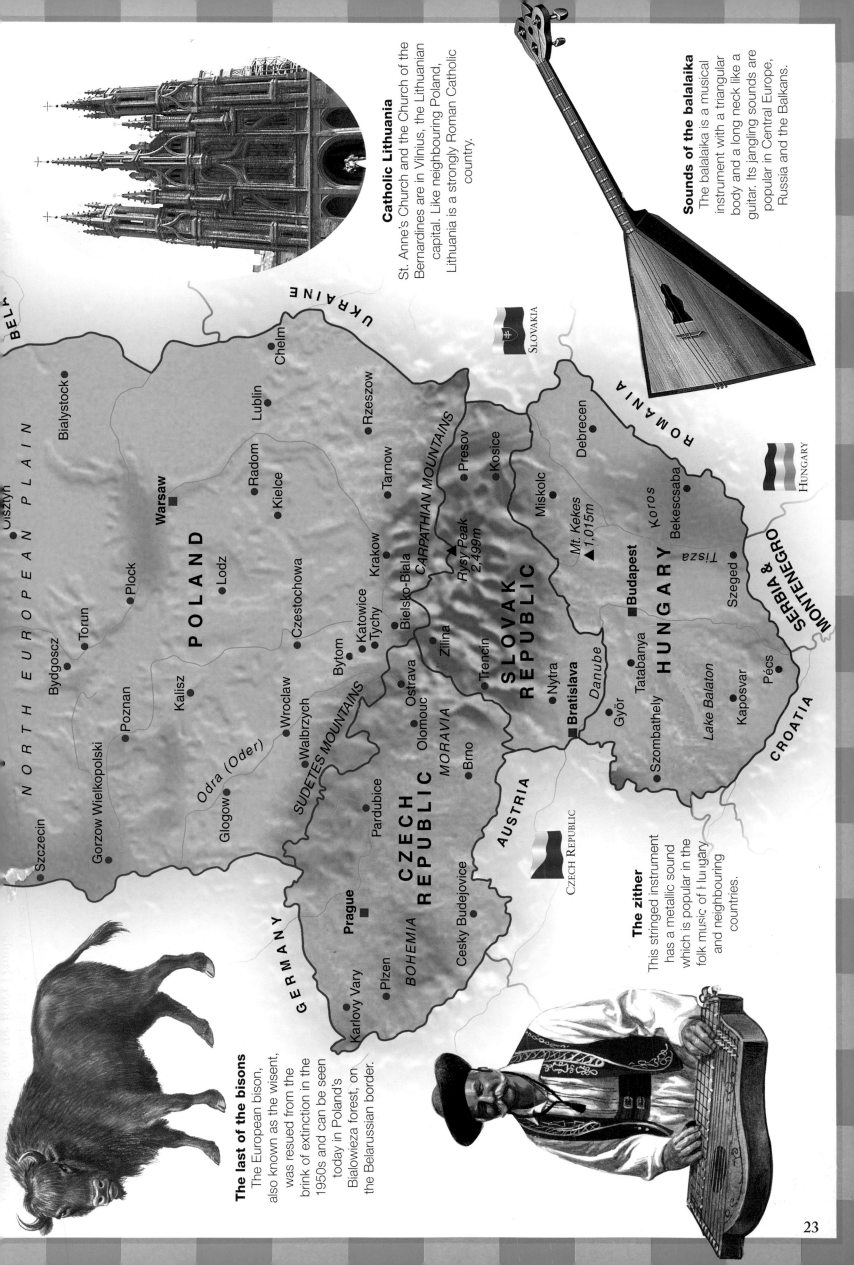

Catholic Lithuania

St. Anne's Church and the Church of the Bernardines are in Vilnius, the Lithuanian capital. Like neighbouring Poland, Lithuania is a strongly Roman Catholic country.

Sounds of the balalaika

The balalaika is a musical instrument with a triangular body and a long neck like a guitar. Its jangling sounds are popular in Central Europe, Russia and the Balkans.

The zither

This stringed instrument has a metallic sound which is popular in the folk music of Hungary and neighbouring countries.

The last of the bisons

The European bison, also known as the wisent, was resued from the brink of extinction in the 1950s and can be seen today in Poland's Bialowieza forest, on the Belarussian border.

BELA

UKRAINE

SLOVAKIA

ROMANIA

HUNGARY

CZECH REPUBLIC

Chelm

Bialystock

Olsztyn

Lublin

Radom

Kielce

Warsaw

Rzeszow

Tarnow

Krakow

Bielsko-Biala

CARPATHIAN MOUNTAINS

Presov

Kosice

Debrecen

Miskolc

Mt. Kekes
▲ 1,015m

Koros

Bekescsaba

Tisza

Szeged

Pécs

Budapest

HUNGARY

SLOVAK REPUBLIC

Nytra

Bratislava

Trencin

Zilina

Tatabanya

Györ

Danube

Szombathely

Lake Balaton

Kaposvar

SERBIA & MONTENEGRO

CROATIA

▲ Rysy Peak
2,499m

AUSTRIA

Plock

Lodz

N O R T H   E U R O P E A N   P L A I N

Szczecin

Gorzow Wielkopolski

Poznan

Bydgoscz

Torun

Kalisz

P O L A N D

Czestochowa

Wroclaw

Walbrzych

Odra (Oder)

Glogow

SUDETES MOUNTAINS

Bytom

Katowice

Tychy

Ostrava

Olomouc

MORAVIA

Brno

CZECH REPUBLIC

Pardubice

BOHEMIA

Cesky Budejovice

GERMANY

Prague

Plzen

Karlovy Vary

CZECH REPUBLIC

BALKANS AND ROMANIA

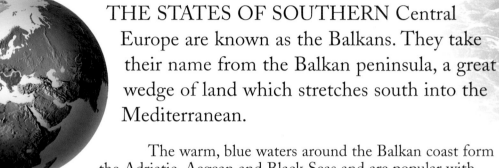

SLOVENIA

N

AUSTRIA

Triglav ▲
2,863 m **Ljubljana**
SLOVENIA

Maribor

Koprivnica

Drava

■ **Zagreb**

CROATIA

Rijeka   Kupa

Pula
● Cres

Prijedor

Bihac

Banja Luka

Losinj   Gospic   **BOSNIA -**
HERZEGOVINA

Zadar ●
Dugi I.

Livno   Zenica

Sibenik ●   **Sarajevo**

Split   Brac

CROATIA   Hvar   Mostar

Vis

Korcula

Lastovo Mljet
Dubrovnik

BOSNIA-
HERZEGOVINA

THE STATES OF SOUTHERN Central
Europe are known as the Balkans. They take
their name from the Balkan peninsula, a great
wedge of land which stretches south into the
Mediterranean.

The warm, blue waters around the Balkan coast form
the Adriatic, Aegean and Black Seas and are popular with
tourists. The region is mountainous, with hot, dry summers.
Winters are severe in the north of the region, but generally mild in the south.
Earthquakes are common. The Balkan countries produce fruit, wines and spirits, dairy
products such as yoghurt and cheese, olives, sunflowers and tobacco.

In the early 1990s the northwest of the region saw bitter fighting as the large
nation of Yugoslavia broke up into separate independent states. These are now named
Slovenia, **Croatia**, **Bosnia-Herzegovina**, **Serbia and Montenegro**, and **Macedonia**
(which is also the name of the northernmost province of Greece). The small and
very poor country of **Albania** also suffered from political unrest and civil war
in the 1990s.

The northeast of the Balkan peninsula is occupied by **Bulgaria**, a
land of fertile farmland to the south of the river Danube, crossed by the
Balkan and Rhodope mountain chains. Its northern neighbour is
Romania, lying around the forested Carpathian mountain range and
the Transylvanian Alps. On the Black Sea coast, the
river Danube forms a marshy delta region.

The Balkan peninsula narrows to the
south, breaking up into the headland of the
Peloponnese and scattered island chains. **Greece**
was the centre of Europe's first great civilizations,
between 4,000 and 2,000 years ago. The rock of
the Acropolis, with its temple, the Parthenon,
still towers above the Greek capital, Athens.

The sunflower crop
Sunflowers are grown in many parts of
southern Europe. Their seeds may be
roasted and eaten as snacks, turned into
cooking oil or used to make margarine.

Off to market
Romanian farmers gather for a cattle fair at
Sugatag. The population as a whole is made up
of Romanians, whose language is linked to the
Latin language of the ancient Roman empire, as
well as Magyars and Gypsies.

Old-fashioned style
Traditional Bulgarian costumes, with
waistcoats, aprons and skirts may still
be seen at many festivals or folk
dances.

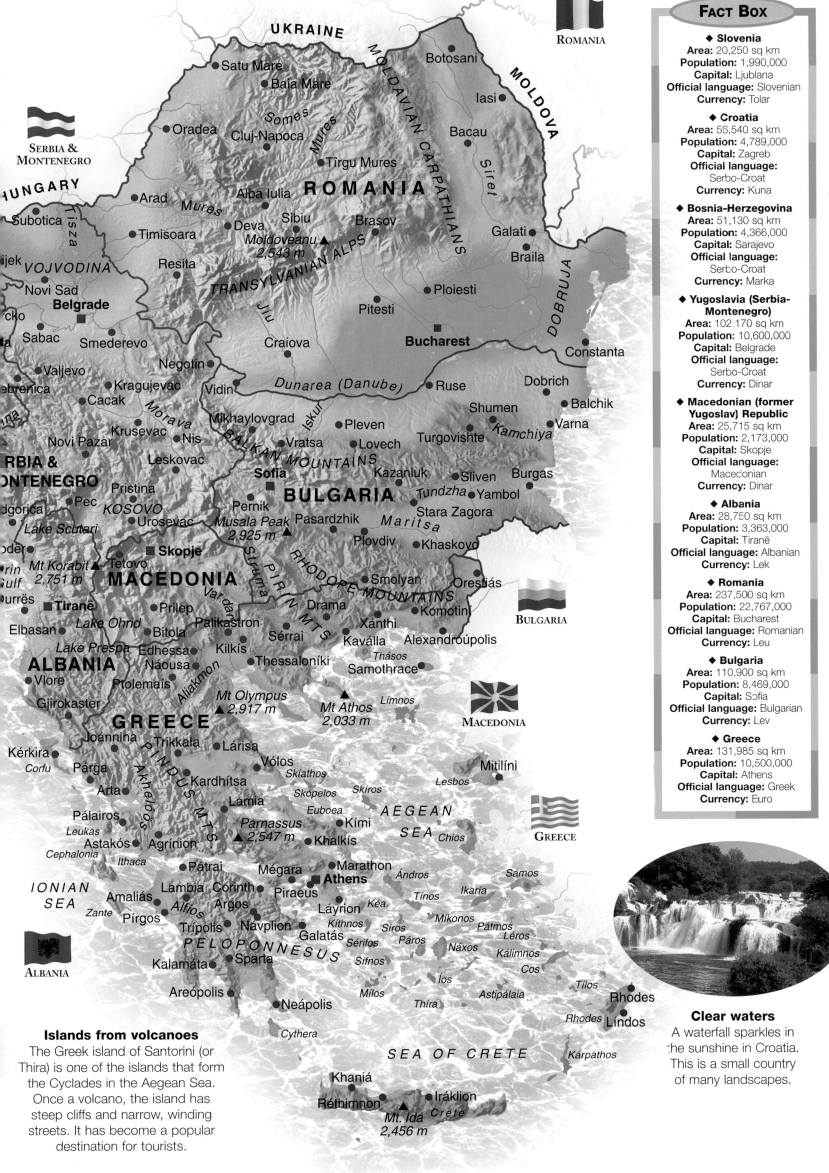

UKRAINE
ROMANIA
MOLDOVA
SERBIA & MONTENEGRO
HUNGARY

Satu Mare
Baia Mare
Somes
Oradea
Cluj-Napoca
Mures
Tîrgu Mures
Botosani
Iasi
Bacau
Siret
MOLDAVIAN CARPATHIANS

Arad
Mures
Alba Iulia
Sibiu
Deva
Moldoveanu ▲ 2,543 m
Brasov
Galati
Braila
ROMANIA
TRANSYLVANIAN ALPS
Timisoara
Resita
Subotica
Tisza
VOJVODINA
Novi Sad
Belgrade
cko
Sabac
Smederevo
Valjevo
brenica
Kragujevac
Cacak
Morava
Krusevac
Novi Pazar
Nis
Leskovac
RBIA & ONTENEGRO
Pristina
Pec
KOSOVO
dgorica
Urosevac
Lake Scutari
oder
rin
Mt Korabit ▲ 2,751 m
Tetovo
ulf
urrës
Skopje
MACEDONIA
Tiranë
Prilep
Lake Ohrid
Bitola
Elbasan
Palikaštron
Lake Prespa
Edhessa
Náousa
Kilkís
ALBANIA
Ptolemaís
Vlore
Aliakmon
Gjirokaster
Mt Olympus ▲ 2,917 m
GREECE
Ioánnina
Trikkala
Lárisa
Kérkira
Corfu
Párga
PINDUS MTS
Vólos
Arta
Kardhítsa
Akhelóos
Pálairos
Lamia
Leukas
Parnassus ▲ 2,547 m
Astakós
Agrínion
Ithaca
Cephalonia
Pátrai
Mégara
IONIAN SEA
Lambia
Corinth
Athens
Zante
Amaliás
Alfiós
Argos
Pírgos
Trípolis
Návplion
Galatás
PELOPONNESUS
Kalamáta
Sparta
Areópolis
Neápolis
Cythera
Khaniá
Réthimnon
Mt. Ida 2,456 m
Iráklion
Crete
SEA OF CRETE

Vidin
Dunarea (Danube)
Mikhaylovgrad
Vratsa
Pleven
Lovech
BALKAN MOUNTAINS
Iskur
Sofia
BULGARIA
Pernik
Pasardzhik
Musala Peak 2,925 m ▲
Struma
PIRIN MTS
Vardar
Drama
RHODOPE MOUNTAINS
Smolyan
Xánthi
Sérrai
Kaválla
Thessaloníki
Thásos
Samothrace
Mt Athos ▲ 2,033 m
Límnos
Mitilíni
Skíathos
Lesbos
Skópelos
Skíros
Euboea
Kími
Khalkís
Chios
AEGEAN SEA
Marathon
Piraeus
Ándros
Sámos
Láyrion
Tínos
Ikaría
Kéa
Míkonos
Kíthnos
Síros
Pátmos
Sérifos
Páros
Léros
Náxos
Kálimnos
Sífnos
Cos
Íos
Mílos
Astipálaia
Thíra
Tílos
Rhodes
Rhodes
Líndos
Kárpathos

Craiova
Pitesti
Ploiesti
Bucharest
Ruse
Dobrich
Balchik
Shumen
Kamchiya
Varna
Turgovishte
Negotin
Kazanluk
Sliven
Burgas
Yambol
Tundzha
Stara Zagora
Maritsa
Plovdiv
Khaskovo
Orestiás
Komotiní
Alexandroúpolis
DOBRUJA
Constanta

FACT BOX

BULGARIA

MACEDONIA

GREECE

ALBANIA

Islands from volcanoes

The Greek island of Santorini (or Thira) is one of the islands that form the Cyclades in the Aegean Sea. Once a volcano, the island has steep cliffs and narrow, winding streets. It has become a popular destination for tourists.

Clear waters

A waterfall sparkles in the sunshine in Croatia. This is a small country of many landscapes.

25

RUSSIA AND ITS NEIGHBOURS

FOR A LARGE PART OF THIS CENTURY all the countries on this map were part of one huge country, the Soviet Union. That nation was formed in the years after November 1917, when communists seized power from the czars. Communist rule ended in 1991 and many of the regions around the former Soviet borders then broke away to become independent countries.

St Basil's Cathedral, Russia
Moscow is famous for the onion-shaped domes of St Basil's Cathedral. It was built in 1555 by Czar Ivan IV to commemorate the defeat of invading Tartars.

The remaining part of the former Soviet Union was renamed the '**Russian Federation**'. It is still by far the largest country in the world, stretching across two continents, Europe and Asia. Eighty percent of the population are Russians, but the rest belong to one of the many other ethnic groups who live in this enormous region.

Northern Russia is a land of tundra, where deep-frozen soil borders the Arctic Ocean. To the south is the great belt of forest known as taiga, whose spruce trees are heavy with snow during the long, bitter winter. Southern Russia and the **Ukraine** have the fertile black earth of the rolling grasslands known as steppes. The lands to the south of Russia's new borders take in warm, fertile valleys, thin grasslands grazed by sheep and goats, deserts and high mountains.

Russia is rich in minerals, oil, natural gas and timber. Its industries were developed in a hurry during the Soviet years, but at great cost to its people and environment. Russia is still an economic giant, producing machinery, textiles, chemicals and vehicles.

BELARUS

UKRAINE

MOLDOVA

GEORGIA

ARMENIA

UZBEKISTAN

AZERBAIJAN

TURKMENISTAN

KYRGYZSTAN

TAJIKISTAN

Franz Josef Land

FINLAND

Murmansk BARENTS SEA

Novaya Zemlya

KARA SEA

Dikso

BELARUS
LITHUANIA
RUSSIA
LATVIA
ESTONIA

L. Ladoga

St Petersburg

L. Onega

N. Dvina

Archangel

Amderma

Salekhard

Yenisey

BELARUS
Minsk
Gomel

Smolensk

Yaroslavl'

Volga

Pechora

Ob'

SIBERIAN LOWLAND

Chernobyl

UKRAINE Kiev

Dnepr

MOLDOVA
Chisinau

Khar'kov

Odessa

Donetsk

Sevastopol

BLACK SEA

Rostov-on-Don

Mt Elbrus
5,642 m

CAUCASUS MTS.

Batumi

TURKEY

GEORGIA
Tbilisi

ARMENIA
Yerevan

AZERBAIJAN
AZER.

Baku

Moscow

Nizhniy Novgorod

Voronezh

Don

Saratov

Volgograd

Astrakhan

Groznyy

Caspian Sea

Kirov

Kazan

Kama

Perm

Ufa

Syzran

Volga

Samara

Magnitogorsk

Ural

Orsk

R U S S

URAL MOUNTAINS

Khanty-Mansiysk

Nizhniy Tagil

Irtysh

Tobol'sk

Yekaterinburg

Chelyabinsk

Ob'

Tom

Omsk

Novosibirsk

Ishim

Astana

KAZAKHSTAN

Irtysh

Karaganda

Semey

SAY

Aral Sea

Syr Dar'ya

TURANIAN PLATEAU

Nukus

Tashauz

UZBEKISTAN

TURKMENISTAN
Ashgabat

Amu Dar'ya

IRAN

Bukhara

Balkhash

Lake Balkhash

Almaty

CHINA

Bishkek
Tashkent KYRGYZSTAN

Dushanbe
TAJIKISTAN

AFGHANISTAN

26

Coarse cotton
Cotton of a tough, coarse grade is grown in Uzbekistan. The country is a major world producer, but in this dry land the cotton crop needs a great deal of irrigation, and this has harmed the environment.

Happy Easter!
Many Russians are Christians belonging to the Eastern Orthodox Church. Traditionally, they exchanged beautifully decorated eggs as gifts at Easter.

RUSSIA

Severnaya Zemlya

New Siberian Islands

Wrangel I.

EAST SIBERIAN SEA

LAPTEV SEA

Os. Lyakhovskiy

Delta of the Lena

Nordvik

Indigirka

Kolyma

KOLYMA LOWLAND

CHERSKIY RANGE

KOLIMA MOUNTAINS

KAMCHATKA PENINSULA

Anadyr'

Commander Is.

VERKHOYANSK RANGE

CENTRAL SIBERIAN PLATEAU

Lena

Yakutsk

ower Tunguska

A

Olekminsk

Lensk

ALDAN MOUNTAINS

DZUGDZHUR

Magadan

Petropavlovsk-Kamchatskiy

SEA OF OKHOTSK

Sakhalin

ngara

STANOVOY RANGE

SIKHOTE ALIN'

Tatarskiy Proliv

Yuzhno-Sakhalinsk

Bratsk

Krasnoyarsk

Lake Baykal

Lena

YABLONOVVY MOUNTAINS

Amur

Khabarovsk

CHINA

Irkutsk

enisey

TS.

Ulan-Ude

MONGOLIA

Vladivostok

KAZAKHSTAN

N

FACT BOX

◆ **Russia**
Area: 17,078,005 sq km
Population: 148,673,000
Capital: Moscow
Official language: Russian
Currency: Rouble

◆ **Belarus**
Area: 208,000 sq km
Population: 10,313,000
Capital: Minsk
Official language: Belarussian
Currency: Rouble

◆ **Ukraine**
Area: 603,700 sq km
Population: 52,194,000
Capital: Kiev
Official language: Ukrainian
Currency: Hryvnya

◆ **Moldova**
Area: 33,7000 sq km
Population: 4,356,000
Capital: Chisinau
Official language: Moldovan
Currency: Leu

◆ **Kazakhstan**
Area: 2,717,300 sq km
Population: 17,035,000
Capital: Astana
Official language: Kazakh
Currency: Tenge

◆ **Armenia**
Area: 30,000 sq km
Population: 3,677,000
Capital: Yerevan
Official language: Armenian
Currencies: Dram, rouble

◆ **Georgia**
Area: 69,700 sq km
Population: 5,471,000
Capital: Tbilisi
Official language: Georgian
Currency: Lari

◆ **Azerbaijan**
Area: 87,000 sq km
Population: 7,398,000
Capital: Baku
Official language: Azeri
Currencies: Manat

◆ **Turkmenistan**
Area: 488,100 sq km
Population: 3,714,000
Capital: Ashgaba
Official language: Turkmen
Currency: Manat

◆ **Uzbekistan**
Area: 447,400 sq km
Population: 21,207,000
Capital: Tashkent
Official language: Uzbek
Currencies: Sum

◆ **Tajikistan**
Area: 143,100 sq km
Population: 5,514,000
Capital: Dushanbe
Official language: Tajik
Currency: Somoni

◆ **Kyrgyzstan**
Area: 198,500 sq km
Population: 4,528,000
Capital: Bishkek
Official language: Kyrgyz
Currency: Sum

In the Caucasus
This woman wears a traditional costume of Dagostan, a part of the Russian Federation which lies between the Caucasus mountains and the Caspian Sea. About 30 different ethnic groups live in this region.

27

NORTH AMERICA

CANADA

FACT BOX

◆ **Canada**
Area: 9,922,385 sq km
Population: 31,000,000
Capital: Ottawa
Official languages: French, English
Currency: Canadian dollar

CANADA is the second largest country in the world and yet it is home to only 30 million people. Most Canadians live in the big cities in the south, such as Toronto, Ottawa, Montréal and Vancouver.

The southern provinces take in the St Lawrence River and Seaway, the Great Lakes, the prairies along the United States border and the foggy coasts of the Atlantic and Pacific Oceans.

The severe climate makes it hard for people to live in the northern wilderness, which stretches into the **Arctic Circle**. Here, a broad belt of spruce forest gives way to bare, deep-frozen soil called tundra, and a maze of islands locked in ice.

Canada's wilderness includes rivers, lakes, coasts and forests. It is home to polar bears and seals, caribou, moose, beavers and loons. It also has valuable resources, providing timber, hydroelectric power and minerals, including oil. **Canada** is a wealthy country.

The first Canadians crossed into North America from Asia long ago, when the two continents were joined by land. They were the Native American peoples and they were followed by the Inuit people of the Arctic. Today these two groups make up only four percent of the population. About 40 percent of Canadians are descended from peoples of the British Isles, especially Scots. People of French descent make up 27 percent, and there are also many people of Eastern European and Asian descent.

Canada has two official languages, French and English. In recent years many people in the French-speaking province of Québec have campaigned to become separate from the rest of Canada.

ARCTIC OCEAN

Melville Island

Banks Island

Prince of Wales Island

BEAUFORT SEA

Victoria Island

ALASKA (U.S.A.)

Dawson

Norman Wells

Great Bear Lake

YUKON TERRITORY

Mackenzie

▲ Mt. Logan 5,951 m

Whitehorse

MACKENZIE MOUNTAINS

Liard

NORTHWEST TERRITORIES

HORN MOUNTAINS

Yellowknife

Dubawnt Laks

Great Slave Lake

Fort Resolution

Fort Smith

ROCKY

CARIBOU MOUNTAINS

Lake Athabasca

BRITISH COLUMBIA

CANADA

Reindeer Lake

Churc

Prince Rupert

COAST MOUNTAINS

Peace

Peace River

ALBERTA

Nels

QUEEN CHARLOTTE ISLANDS

Prince George

MOUNTAINS

Edmonton

N. Saskatchewan

MANITOB

Fraser

Red Deer

Prince Albert

Lake

Kamloops

Lake Winnip

Winnipegosis

Vancouver Island

Caigary

Saskatoon

Vancouver

Medicine Hat

SASKATCHEWAN

Lake Manitoba

Victoria

S. Saskatchewan

Regina

Winnipe

UNITED STATES OF AMERICA

Wheat Harvest
Large combine harvesters cross the Canadian prairies. These are natural grasslands which are now largely given over to wheat and cattle production. They occupy parts of Manitoba, Saskatchewan and Alberta and stretch across the border into the northern United States.

Sugar maple
The maple leaf is the symbol on the Canadian national flag. Sap from the tree is boiled up to make a very popular food product, maple syrup, which is poured over pancakes and waffles. The syrup was first invented long ago by native peoples of the St Lawrence valley.

Arctic travel
In the ice and snow of the Canadian Arctic, travelling can be difficult. Snowmobiles, rather like motorcycles with skis instead of wheels, have now mostly replaced the traditional dog sleds.

Toronto, Ontario view over city
The CN Tower soars 553 metres above Canada's largest city, Toronto. This is a centre of business and industry built on the shores of Lake Ontario. It is also the capital of the vast province of Ontario.

CANADA

Ice hockey
Fast and hard, ice hockey is one of Canada's most popular spectator sports. The game was invented in Canada, its rules being drawn up in Montréal in 1879. There are two teams of six skaters. Both Canadian and US teams compete within two major leagues.

LINCOLN SEA

esmere sland

von Island

BAFFIN BAY

Baffin Island

Davis Strait

FOXE BASIN

LABRADOR SEA

Southampton Island

Hudson Strait

Coats Island

Mansel Island

Ungava Peninsula

HUDSON BAY

urchill

Feuilles

Belcher Islands

La Grande Rivière

Severn

JAMES BAY

Akimiski Island

OTISH MOUNTAINS

• Goose Bay

NEWFOUNDLAND

Péribonca

• Gander

Newfoundland • St John s

Albany

ONTARIO

QUEBEC

St. Lawrence

Anticosti Island

Gulf of St. Lawrence

PRINCE EDWARD ISLAND

NEW BRUNSWICK

• Charlottetown

NOVA SCOTIA

Lake Nipigon

Quebec •

St John •

Fredericton •

• Halifax

Thunder Bay

Montreal •

Ottawa

ATLANTIC OCEAN

Lake Superior

Georgian Bay

Lake Huron

Toronto •

Lake Ontario

N

Hamilton •

• Niagara Falls

Windsor •

Lake Erie

USA

THE UNITED STATES OF AMERICA

make up a huge country, which crosses no less than eight time zones. It extends from the Pacific to the Atlantic Oceans, from Canada south to Mexico.

The modern nation was formed by colonists from Europe, who from the 1500s onwards seized and settled the lands of the Native American peoples. In 1776 the British colonies in the east declared their independence, and the new country grew rapidly during the 1800s as it gained territory from France, Mexico and Russia. Today, in addition to the small Native American population, there are Americans whose ancestors came from all over Europe, including Britain, Ireland, Scandinavia, Germany, Russia and Italy. There are African Americans, whose ancestors were brought to America as slaves. There are Hispanics, people of Spanish ancestry. There are many Asian Americans, whose ancestors came from India, Pakistan, China, Japan, Korea and Vietnam. All are citizens of the United States.

The nation today is a federation of 50 states, which have the power to pass many of their own laws. The federal capital is at Washington, in the District of Columbia (DC). Here is the Congress, made up of a Senate and a House of Representatives, and the White House, the home of the US presidents.

The American economy is the most powerful in the world. The country is rich in minerals, including oil, coal and iron ore. American companies produce computers and software, aircraft, cars and processed foods. There are also many large banks and finance companies. America leads in space exploration and technology. The films and television programmes produced in America are watched by people in many countries around the world.

FACT BOX

◆ **United States of America**
Area: 9,363,130 sq km
Population: 286,000,000
Capital: Washington DC
Official language: English
Currency: US dollar

The woods of Vermont
Vermont is in New England and nicknamed the Green Mountain State. It is famous for its brilliant foliage in the autumn or fall.

Monument Valley, Arizona
This spectacular landscape is sculpted by nature and is formed of red sandstone. There are many Wild West legends rooted here.

The Bald Eagle
This is America's national bird. It has a white head, and a wingspan of up to 2 metres. Its natural habitat is by lakes and rivers, and for food it preys mainly on fish and rodents.

THE UNITED STATES OF AMERICA

MAINE
Bangor
Augusta
Burlington
VERMONT
NEW HAMPSHIRE
Portland
Montpelier
NEW YORK
Concord
MASSACHUSETTS
Cape Cod
Rochester
Syracuse
Boston
Albany
Hartford
Providence
RHODE ISLAND
Buffalo
CONNECTICUT
Scranton
New York City
Erie
PENNSYLVANIA
NEW JERSEY
Cleveland
Philadelphia
Trenton
Akron
Harrisburg
Dover
Toledo
Pittsburgh
Baltimore
DELAWARE
OHIO
Columbus
WASHINGTON D.C.
Annapolis
MARYLAND
Dayton
WEST VIRGINIA
Chesapeake Bay
Cincinnati
Richmond
Ohio
Charleston
VIRGINIA
Louisville
Frankfort
Norfolk
Evansville
Lexington
Roanoke
KENTUCKY
Greensboro
Cape Hatteras
Paducah
Knoxville
Raleigh
Nashville
Winston-Salem
NORTH CAROLINA
Charlotte
TENNESSEE
Chattanooga
Greenville
Wilmington
Memphis
SOUTH CAROLINA
Cape Fear
Tennessee
Alabama
Columbia
Tupelo
Birmingham
Atlanta
Augusta
Charleston
Little Rock
Macon
Arkansas
Greenville
Savannah
ALABAMA
Columbus
GEORGIA
Meridian
Montgomery
Shreveport
Jackson
Albany
LOUISIANA
Jacksonville
MISSISSIPPI
Mobile
St. Augustine
Alexandria
Biloxi
Tallahassee
Daytona Beach
Baton Rouge
Pensacola
Cape Canaveral
New Orleans
Orlando
Mississippi Delta
Tampa
FLORIDA
St. Petersburg
Lake Okeechobee
West Palm Beach
Fort Myers
GULF OF MEXICO
Miami
Florida Keys
Key West
Straits of Florida

Grand Forks
MINNESOTA
Lake Superior
Duluth
Marquette
Lake Huron
ORTH AKOTA
amestown
nark
Fargo
Red
St. Cloud
WISCONSIN
Green Bay
MICHIGAN
Aberdeen
Minneapolis
St Paul
La Crosse
Grand Rapids
Missouri
James
Sioux Falls
IOWA
Milwaukee
Madison
Rockford
Detroit
Lansing
Windsor
Lake Erie
OUTH AKOTA
Cedar Rapids
Chicago
Gary
EBRASKA
Norfolk
Sioux City
Davenport
INDIANA
rand Island
Omaha
Des Moines
Peoria
ILLINOIS
Indianapolis
Platte
Lincoln
Springfield
Missouri
Kansas City
Jefferson City
St. Louis
Louisville
Abilene
Topeka
MISSOURI
Salina
ANSAS
Hutchinson
Joplin
Springfield
Wichita
Tulsa
Cimarron
ARKANSAS
OKLAHOMA
Fort Smith
Oklahoma City
Arkansas
Red River
Wichita Falls
Texarkana
Brazos
Dallas
ene
Fort Worth
Waco
Alexandria
TEXAS
Angelo
Austin
Beaumont
Houston
Port Arthur
San Antonio
Galveston
Laredo
Brownsville
La Crosse
Jefferson City

N

31

The northeastern United States have a mild climate, although winter snowfall can be heavy and summers can be warm. Inland from the rocks and stormy shores of the Atlantic coast are the woodlands of the New England region, which turn to every shade of red and gold in the autumn. Here there are broad rivers and neat little towns dating back to the days of the early settlers, as well as the historic city of Boston, Massachusetts. In the far north the Great Lakes mark the border with Canada. On this border are the spectacular Niagara Falls, a major tourist attraction which also provides valuable hydroelectric power. The Appalachian mountain ranges run for 2,400 kilometres from north to south, through the eastern United States.

The northeastern United States include centres of industry and mining, and large cities with gleaming skyscrapers, sprawling suburbs, road and rail networks. New York City, centred around the island of Manhattan, is the business capital of the United States and also a lively centre of arts and entertainment. To many people, New York City is a symbol of America – fast-moving and energetic, a melting pot of different peoples and cultures. The northern city of Detroit is a centre of the motor industry, and Chicago, on the windy shores of Lake Michigan, is another bustling city of skyscrapers, and an important centre of business and manufacture.

Travelling south from the Delaware River and the great city of Philadelphia, you come to the federal District of Columbia, the site of Washington, capital city of the United States. Approaching the American South, you pass into warmer country where tobacco and cotton are grown in the red earth. The long peninsula of Florida extends southwards into the Caribbean Sea, fringed by sandy islands called keys. Along the Gulf coast the climate is hot and very humid, with creeks known as bayous and tangled swamps which are home to alligators.

Hurricanes are common in late summer and autumn. New Orleans, the home of jazz, has many picturesque old buildings with wrought-iron verandas. It lies 170 kilometres above the mouth of the Mississippi River, which together with the mighty Missouri drains the centre of the continent. Texas is a huge state which borders Mexico along the Rio Grande. Dry and dusty, it makes its living from cattle ranching and oil.

Prairies once covered the great plains of the Midwest, the home of vast herds of bison or buffalo. Today the grasslands are largely given over to farming vegetable crops and grain, or to cattle ranching. The wheat and maize produced on the Prairies have led to them being called the 'breadbasket of the world'.

Barren, stony 'badlands' rise towards the rugged Rocky Mountain ranges, which form the backbone of the United States as they stretch from the Canadian border south to Mexico. Southwards and westwards again there are large areas of burning desert, salt flats and canyons, where over the ages the rocks have been worn into fantastic shapes by wind and water. In places the Grand Canyon of Arizona is 24 kilometres wide and two kilometres deep, a spectacular gorge cut out by the waters of the Colorado River.

Jambalaya!
Rice, seafood, green peppers and hot spices make up this delicious dish from New Orleans, in Louisiana. The people of this city include many of French and African descent, and this shows in its cooking.

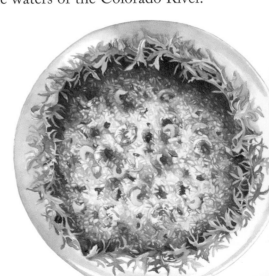

The Statue of Liberty
This huge monument, a gift from the people of France in 1886, was the first sight of America for many immigrants.

Badwater, in California's harsh Death Valley, is the lowest point in the United States, 86 metres below sea level.

The Sierra, Cascade and Coast ranges run parallel with the beautiful Pacific coast. The warm beaches, pines and gigantic redwood trees of California stretch northwards to the ferny forests of Oregon and Washington State, which is rainy and cool. Irrigation has made it possible to farm large areas of California, which produce citrus fruits and grape vines. Major cities of the west include Los Angeles, which takes in the world-famous film studios of Hollywood; beautiful San Francisco, set on a wide bay which can be warm and sparkling blue or shrouded in cool sea-fog; and the busy northern port of Seattle.

The United States has a northern outpost in oil-rich Alaska, its largest state. Alaska was purchased from Russia in 1867. Bordered by Canada, the Alaskan wilderness stretches into the remote Arctic, a deep frozen land of mountains and tundra.

Its islands are inhabited by large grizzly bears and its waters by schools of migrating whales.

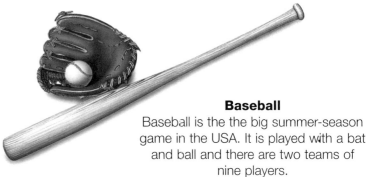

Baseball
Baseball is the the big summer-season game in the USA. It is played with a bat and ball and there are two teams of nine players.

Mount McKinley, at 6,194 metres, is the highest point not just in the United States, but in all of North America.

Far to the west, in the Pacific Ocean, the Hawaiian Islands are also part of the United States. Tourists come here to enjoy the warm climate and the surf and to see the islands' spectacular volcanoes.

The United States also governs or has special links with various other territories, such as American Samoa, the Northern Marianas and the Midway Islands in the Pacific Ocean. Puerto Rico and the US Virgin Islands in the Caribbean are also governed by the United States.

The United States has close economic links with its neighbours, Canada and Mexico, through the North American Free Trade Agreement of 1994. It is also a member of many other international groupings, such as the the North Atlantic Treaty Organization (NATO), a military alliance which links it with Western and Central Europe.

As the world's most powerful country, the influence of the United States is to be seen in many other lands. Films and television programmes have made the American way of life influential around the world. Hamburgers and soft drinks are now bought in many other countries. American blues and jazz has influenced all kinds of popular music and American slang is used by people around the world.

Manhattan
On Manhattan island, the heart of New York City, architects have built the city's tallest buildings. After 2001, when a terrorist attack destroyed the twin towers of the World Trade Center, the skyline was again dominated by the 1930s Empire State Building.

Cops and crime
American policemen and detectives fight city crime. Their work has been made famous around the world by countless films and television series.

Heart of the nation
The impressive Capitol building is at the centre of Washington, District of Columbia. It is used by the United States Congress and was constructed between 1851 and 1863.

Blast-off!
The space shuttle leaves Earth on another mission. The United States has been a pioneer of space exploration since the 1960s.

MEXICO, CENTRAL AMERICA & THE CARIBBEAN

Ancient stones
Many great civilizations developed in ancient times in Mexico and Central America. Statues like this, called chacmools, were used during human sacrifices.

MEXICO is a large, mountainous country with a tropical climate. It stretches southwards from the Rio Grande on the United States border, and meets the Pacific Ocean in the west and the Gulf of Mexico in the east.

Mexico is a land of deserts, forests and volcanoes, dotted with the spectacular ruins of ancient Native American civilizations, such as the Maya, Toltec and Aztec. Mexico City, built on the site of an ancient Aztec city, is a vast, sprawling centre of population.

To the south, **Central America** narrows to a thin strip of land called the isthmus of Panama. Guatemala, Belize, Honduras, El Salvador, Nicaragua, Costa Rica and Panama are all small nations that live mostly by farming tropical crops such as bananas, coffee and sugar-cane. Many Mexicans and Central Americans are of Native American, Spanish or mixed descent.

Tijuana
Mexicali
Ensenada
Gulf of California
Baja California
Cedros I.
UNITED STATES OF AMERICA
Ciudad Juárez
Hermosillo
Chihuahua
SIERRA MADRE
Rio Grande
Rio Bravo del Norte
SIERRA MADRE
Torreón
Monterrey
Matamoros
Saltillo
Culiacán
Durango
La Paz
San Luis Potosí
Tampico
Aguascalientes
Guadalajara
León
Cape Corrientes
L. de Chapala
Manzanillo
MEXICO City
Veracruz
MEXICO
Puebla
Orizaba 5,700 m
Balsas
Coatzacoalcas
Acapulco
Oaxaca

GULF OF MEXICO

Havana
CUBA
CUBA
Yucatán Channel
Isla de la Juventud
Cayman Islands
Mérida
Cancún
Campeche
Yucatán Peninsula
Bay of Campeche
Terminos Lagoon
Villahermosa
Belize City
BELIZE
Belmopan
BELIZE
GUATEMALA
HONDURAS
Gulf of Tehuantapec
Tegucigalpa
Guatemala City
San Salvador
NICARAGUA
EL SALVADOR
Lake Nicaragua
Managua
Mosqu Gul
San José
COSTA RICA

PACIFIC OCEAN

N

MECIXO

GUATEMALA

EL SALVADOR

NICARAGUA

COSTA RICA

Birds of a feather
The quetzal is a brilliantly coloured bird. It lives in rainforests from southern Mexico to Panama, where it feeds on berries and fruits.

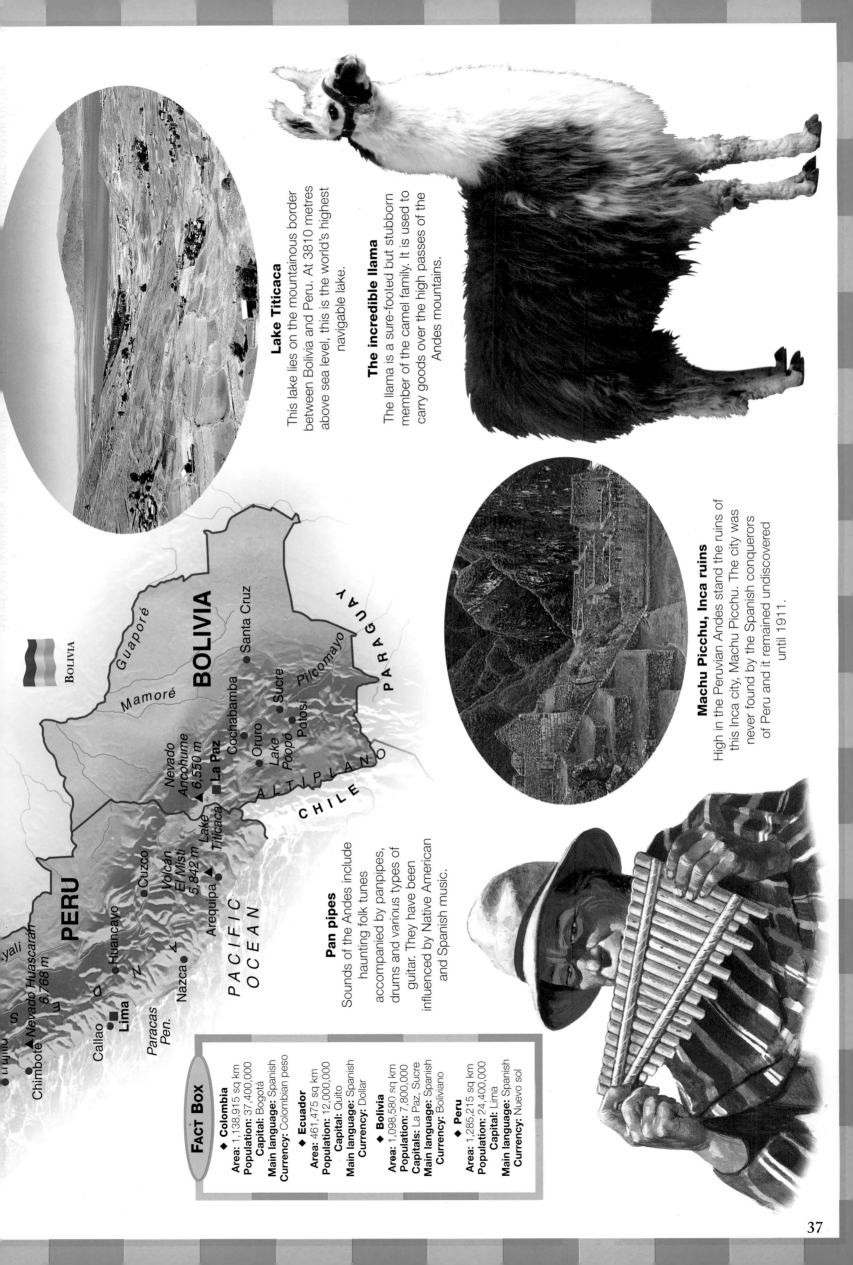

Lake Titicaca

This lake lies on the mountainous border between Bolivia and Peru. At 3810 metres above sea level, this is the world's highest navigable lake.

The incredible llama

The llama is a sure-footed but stubborn member of the camel family. It is used to carry goods over the high passes of the Andes mountains.

Machu Picchu, Inca ruins

High in the Peruvian Andes stand the ruins of this Inca city, Machu Picchu. The city was never found by the Spanish conquerors of Peru and it remained undiscovered until 1911.

Pan pipes

Sounds of the Andes include haunting folk tunes accompanied by panpipes, drums and various types of guitar. They have been influenced by Native American and Spanish music.

BOLIVIA

PERU

BOLIVIA

Guaporé

Mamoré

Santa Cruz

Nevado Ancohune
6,550 m

Cochabamba

La Paz
Oruro
Lake
Poopó
Sucre
Potosí

Pilcomayo

P A R A G U A Y

ALTIPLANO

CHILE

Lake
Titicaca

Cuzco

Volcán
El Misti
5,842 m

Arequipa

Huancayo

Nazca

PACIFIC
OCEAN

Paracas
Pen.

Callao
Lima

Chimbote
Nevado Huascarán
6,768 m

yali

Fact Box

◆ Colombia
Area: 1,138,915 sq km
Population: 37,400,000
Capital: Bogotá
Main language: Spanish
Currency: Colombian peso

◆ Ecuador
Area: 461,475 sq km
Population: 12,000,000
Capital: Quito
Main language: Spanish
Currency: Dollar

◆ Bolivia
Area: 1,098,580 sq km
Population: 7,800,000
Capitals: La Paz, Sucre
Main language: Spanish
Currency: Boliviano

◆ Peru
Area: 1,285,215 sq km
Population: 24,400,000
Capital: Lima
Main language: Spanish
Currency: Nuevo sol

Netherlands Antilles

Gulf of Venezuela

Maracaibo

Lake Maracaibo

Caracas

Barcelona

Port of Spain

TRINIDAD & TOBAGO

ANDES MTS.

LLANOS

Orinoco Delta

Orinoco

Pico Bolívar 5,002 m

VENEZUELA

Angel Falls

Georgetown

GUYANA

Paramaribo

SURINAM

Cayenne

FRENCH GUIANA

COLOMBIA

GUIANA HIGHLANDS

Orinoco

Branco

VENEZUELA

Pico da Neblina 3014 m

Negro

Japurá

Macapá

Marajó Bay

Marajó I.

Belèm

São Marcos Bay

São Luis

FRENCH GUIANA

Amazon

Manaus

Santarém

Tocantins

Teresina

S E L V A S

Madeira

Tapajós

Xingu

Juruá

Purus

Aripuanã

Araguaia

Parnaiba

Jiparaná

Rio Branco

Arinos

BRAZIL

Sobradinho Reservoir

PERU

SERRA DOS PARECIS Guaporé

BOLIVIA

MATO GROSSO PLATEAU

Cuiabá

Brasília

Goiânia

B R A Z I L I A N   H I G H L A N D S

Uberlandia

Campo Grande

Belo Horizonte

Paraná

Campos

São Paulo

Santos

Rio de Janeiro

Cape Frio

PARAGUAY

Itaipu Res.

Itguaçu Falls

SERRA DO MAR

Curitiba

BRAZIL

Florianópolis

ARGENTINA

Uruguay

Santa Maria

Pôrto Alegre

Patos Lagoon

URUGUAY

Mirim Lake

N

Coffee beans

Brazil is the world's biggest producer of coffee. The crop is mostly grown on large estates in the south and is exported worldwide.

Rio panorama

A huge statue of Christ stands high above the Brazilian port of Rio de Janeiro.

BRAZIL AND ITS NEIGHBOURS

BRAZIL is South America's largest nation. It includes grasslands, fertile plateaus and dry areas of scrub.

About a third of the country is taken up by tropical rainforests. All kinds of rare plants, parrots, snakes and monkeys live in these dense, dripping forests, which are under threat from road-builders, farmers, miners and loggers. The forests are crossed by hundreds of rivers, which drain into the wide, muddy waters of the Amazon, one of the world's two longest rivers. The river basin of the Amazon is the world's largest, covering 7,045,000 square kilometres.

Most Brazilians live in the big cities of the Atlantic coast, such as Rio de Janeiro and São Paulo. The country has rich resources, but many of the population are poor people who live in shacks built on the outskirts of the city. Brasília, with its broad avenues and high-rise buildings, was specially built as the country's new capital city in the 1960s.

To the northeast of Brazil, on the Caribbean coast, is **Venezuela**. This land, crossed by the Orinoco River, includes rainforests, high mountains and the tropical grassy plains of the Llanos. The beautiful Angel Falls (the world's highest at 979 metres) provide hydroelectric power, while Lake Maracaibo, in the northwest, is rich in oil.

The three other countries on the Caribbean coast are **Guyana**, **Surinam** and **French Guiana**. The first was once a British colony, the second was a Dutch colony and the third is still an overseas department governed by France. Most people live in the humid regions of the coast, while the rainforests and mountains of the remote south are more sparsely populated. Crops include sugar-cane, coffee, rice and bananas. An important mineral is bauxite, used in the making of aluminium.

Many different ethnic groups live in the region as a whole, including Native American peoples who have had to struggle to survive ever since Europeans invaded the region in the 1500s. The population of northern South America also includes many people of Asian, African, European and mixed descent, with ancestors from Spain, Portugal, Italy, Germany, France, Netherlands and Britain.

Rainforest creatures
The vast forests, which are drained by the River Amazon, support all kinds of wildlife, such as this brightly coloured macaw. Sadly, many species are threatened by the clearance of the forests by farmers and illegal traders in wildlife.

Fishing for a living
A fishing crew check their tackle as children play on the beach. This scene is near Salvador, capital of the tropical Bahía region in northeastern Brazil.

Yanomami hunters
About 13,000 Yanomami people live in Venezuela and another 8,000 in Brazil. They live by hunting, fishing and growing food in the rainforest.

FACT BOX

◆ Brazil
Area: 8,511,965 sq km
Population: 160,300,000
Capital: Brasília
Main language: Portuguese
Currency: Real

◆ Venezuela
Area: 912,045 sq km
Population: 22,600,000
Capital: Caracas
Main language: Spanish
Currency: Bolívar

◆ Guyana
Area: 214,970 sq km
Population: 800,000
Capital: Georgetown
Main language: English
Currency: Guyana dollar

◆ Surinam
Area: 163,820 sq km
Population: 446,000
Capital: Paramaribo
Official language: Dutch
Currency: Surinam guilder

◆ French Guiana
Area: 91,000 sq km
Population: 300,000
Capital: Cayenne
Main language: French
Currency: Euro

Fortaleza

Natal

SERTÃO

Recife

São Francisco

Maceió

Salvador

ARGENTINA AND ITS NEIGHBOURS

THE SOUTHERN PART of South America stretches from the hot and humid Gran Chaco region to the cold and stormy waters of Tierra del Fuego and Cape Horn.

The largest country of this region is **Argentina**. Its highly populated capital is Buenos Aires on the river Plate. More than eight out of every ten Argentineans are city dwellers. However it was the country's cattle-farming regions – the Pampa grasslands and the northeast – that in the last 150 years brought wealth to the country and attracted large numbers of settlers from Europe. Argentina's western borders follow the high peak of the Andes range, which reach their highest point at Cerro Aconcagua (6,959 metres above sea level). To the south are the windswept plateaus of Patagonia, largely given over to sheep farming. The port of Ushuaia is the southernmost town in the world.

Northwards from Buenos Aires, across the river Plate, lies Montevideo, capital of **Uruguay**. This is another country which raises cattle and sheep, and whose rich grasslands and mild climate attracted European settlers. Neighbouring **Paraguay** is far from the coast. Most of its people farm the hills and plains of the east. Few live in the hot wilderness of the Gran Chaco.

To the west of the Andes is **Chile**, which covers a long and narrow area. Here is one of the driest regions on Earth, the Atacama desert. It also includes fertile orchards and productive vineyards, the big city of Santiago and the spectacular glaciers of the southern Andes. Spanish is spoken throughout the region, and some Native American languages such as Guaraní may also be heard.

Armadillo

The head and body of the armadillo is covered by an armour of plates made of horny and bony material. These usually nocturnal animals feed mainly on insects and rest in a burrow by day.

Paraná River, Paraguay

Separating Paraguay and Argentina, the Paraná River flows some 4,500 km. The English explorer Sebastian Cabot was the first to sail up it in 1526.

BRAZIL

PARAGUAY

Cuidad del Este

Concepción

Asunción

Alto Paraná

Posadas

Paraná

Verde

Pilcomayo

Bermejo

Formosa

Resistencia

Corrientes

Salado

Parana

MESOPOTAMIA

URUGUAY

Salto

Paysandú

Negro

Concordia

Paraná

Santa Fe

Rosario

Mar Chiquito

Córdoba

Río Cuarto

PARAGUAY

BOLIVIA

Salta

San Miguel de Tucumán

Santiago del Estero

Catamarca

La Rioja

SIERRA DE CORDOBA

S

N

A

I

L

Ojos del Salado
6,880 m

Copiapó

San Juan

Mendoza

Aconcagua
6,959 m

Santiago

Valparaiso

Coquimbo

Pta. Lengua de Vaca

ATACAMA DESERT

Arica

Iquique

Calama

Antofagasta

CHILE

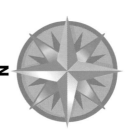

Turkish women
These women are from the port of Kas in southern Turkey. They are kneading dough and making pastry. Many Muslim women cover their heads with scarves or full veils.

ASIA

SOUTHWEST ASIA

SOUTHWEST ASIA IS SOMETIMES described as the Near East or the Middle East. Its peoples include Greek Cypriots, Turks, Jews, Arabs, Kurds and Iranians.

The region has seen many political disputes and wars in recent years – between Greeks and Turks on Cyprus, between Palestinian Arabs and Jews in Israel, between Iraqi and Iranians and between Iraqui and Kuwaiti Arabs. The Kurds, whose homeland is occupied by **Iraq**, **Iran** and **Turkey**, have also been at the centre of conflict.

It was in Southwest Asia that the world's first civilizations grew up, between the rivers Tigris and Euphrates, over 6,000 years ago. The region later gave birth to three world faiths – Judaism, Christianity and Islam. In the days of the Roman empire the Jews were scattered from their homeland, and over the centuries their culture spread to Spain, Central and Eastern Europe and the Americas. Arab armies and traders took the Islamic faith into Africa and Spain, and Arab scholars made great advances in mathematics and astronomy. From the 1500s the Turks established a great empire which stretched from Central Europe to the Indian Ocean.

Southwest Asia includes vast deserts, in the Arabian peninsula and in eastern Iran. It also takes in fertile plains, the marshes of southern Iraq and mountain ranges of Turkey and Iran. The north of the region borders the Black Sea and the Caspian Sea, grassy steppes and the Caucasus mountains. To the east lies Afghanistan, Pakistan and the Indian sub-continent.

The region's most valuable resource is oil, which brings wealth to the governments of the lands around the Persian Gulf. However many ordinary people of Southwest Asia remain poor, living by herding goats, sheep or camels. In Israel and some other regions irrigation has made it possible to grow crops in harsh, dry environments. Oranges, dates, grapes and many kinds of nuts are grown in the region.

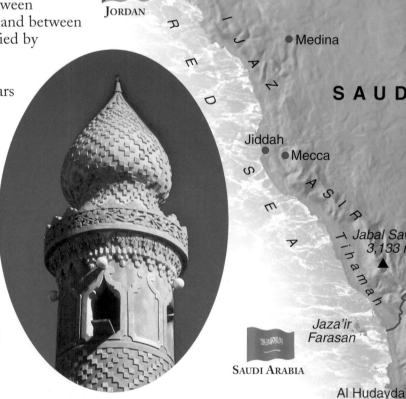

A summons to prayer
Mosques, like this one in Kuwait, have tall towers called minarets. From here, faithful Muslims are called to prayer. This message is often broadcast from loudspeakers. Muslims are expected to pray five times a day.

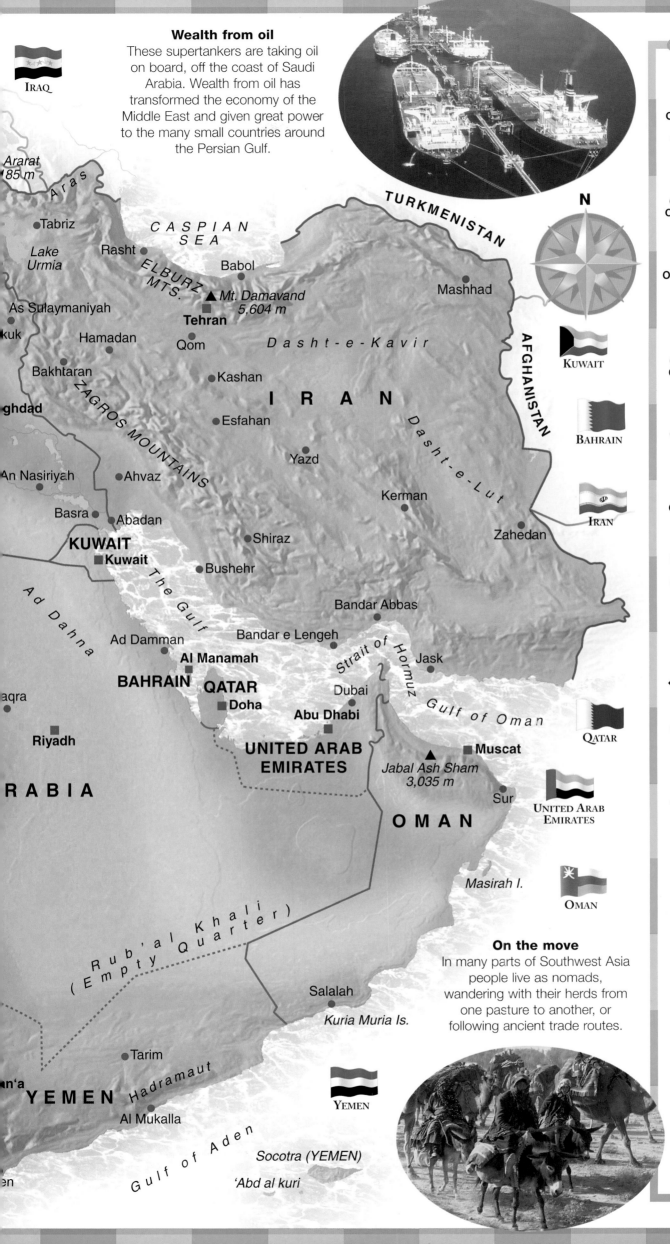

Wealth from oil
These supertankers are taking oil on board, off the coast of Saudi Arabia. Wealth from oil has transformed the economy of the Middle East and given great power to the many small countries around the Persian Gulf.

IRAQ

TURKMENISTAN

N

Ararat
85 m

Aras

Tabriz

*C A S P I A N
S E A*

Rasht

*Lake
Urmia*

Babol

*ELBURZ
MTS.*

Mashhad

As Sulaymaniyah

▲ Mt. Damavand
5,604 m

Tehran

kuk

Hamadan

Qom

D a s h t - e - K a v i r

AFGHANISTAN

ghdad

Bakhtaran

Kashan

ZAGROS MOUNTAINS

I R A N

KUWAIT

An Nasiriyah

Esfahan

D a s h t - e - L u t

Ahvaz

Yazd

BAHRAIN

Basra

Abadan

Kerman

IRAN

KUWAIT

■ Kuwait

Shiraz

Zahedan

The Gulf

Bushehr

Ad Dahna

Bandar Abbas

Ad Damman

Bandar e Lengeh

Strait of Hormuz

Jask

Al Manamah

Dubai

Gulf of Oman

BAHRAIN **QATAR**

■ **Doha**

Abu Dhabi

QATAR

aqra

**UNITED ARAB
EMIRATES**

■ **Muscat**

Riyadh

UNITED ARAB
EMIRATES

▲
*Jabal Ash Sham
3,035 m*

Sur

O M A N

RABIA

OMAN

*(R u b ' a l K h a l i
E m p t y Q u a r t e r)*

Masirah I.

Salalah

On the move
In many parts of Southwest Asia people live as nomads, wandering with their herds from one pasture to another, or following ancient trade routes.

Kuria Muria Is.

Tarim

Hadramaut

n'a

YEMEN

Y E M E N

Al Mukalla

Gulf of Aden

Socotra (YEMEN)

'Abd al kuri

INDIA AND ITS NEIGHBOURS

SOUTHERN ASIA stretches south into the Indian Ocean, forming a landmass so large that it sometimes called the 'sub-continent'. Its northern limits are marked by the Himalaya and Karakoram mountain ranges. These include many of the world's highest peaks and reach 8,848 metres above sea level at Everest, on Nepal's border with China.

The ranges pass through eastern Afghanistan, the Kashmir region on the border of India and Pakistan, India itself and the small mountain kingdoms of **Nepal** and **Bhutan**. Melting snows flow south from the mountains to form the five great rivers of the Punjab and also the mighty Ganges, which winds across the fertile plains of northern India before crossing Bangladesh into a maze of waterways around the Bay of Bengal. This area suffers from devastating floods.

Central and southern **India** form a triangular plateau called the Deccan, fringed on the east and west by the mountainous Ghats. These slopes are forested, catching the full force of the monsoon winds which bring rains from the Indian Ocean. For most of the year India is extremely hot and dry. Indian Ocean nations include the beautiful, tropical island of **Sri Lanka** and a chain of very low coral islands, the **Maldives**.

Advanced civilizations had developed around the river Indus by about 2500BC, and great religions grew up in India over the ages, including Hinduism, Buddhism and Sikhism. Invaders and traders brought Islam to the region. India today is a fascinating mixture of cultures, with over 800 different languages and dialects. There are many different customs, dress and foods. Spicy dishes from India are now popular everywhere.

The Indian sub-continent has a vast population, with many hungry mouths to feed. Many people make their living by farming, growing wheat, rice, millet, sugarcane, coconut and tea. Most industries are based in the highly populated cities of India and Pakistan.

Himalayan peaks

Breathtaking Mount Makalu, on the border between Nepal and China, rises to 8,470 metres above sea level. About 88 per cent of the world's mountains over 7,300 metres rise within the Himalaya-Karakoram ranges, many of them in the kingdom of Nepal.

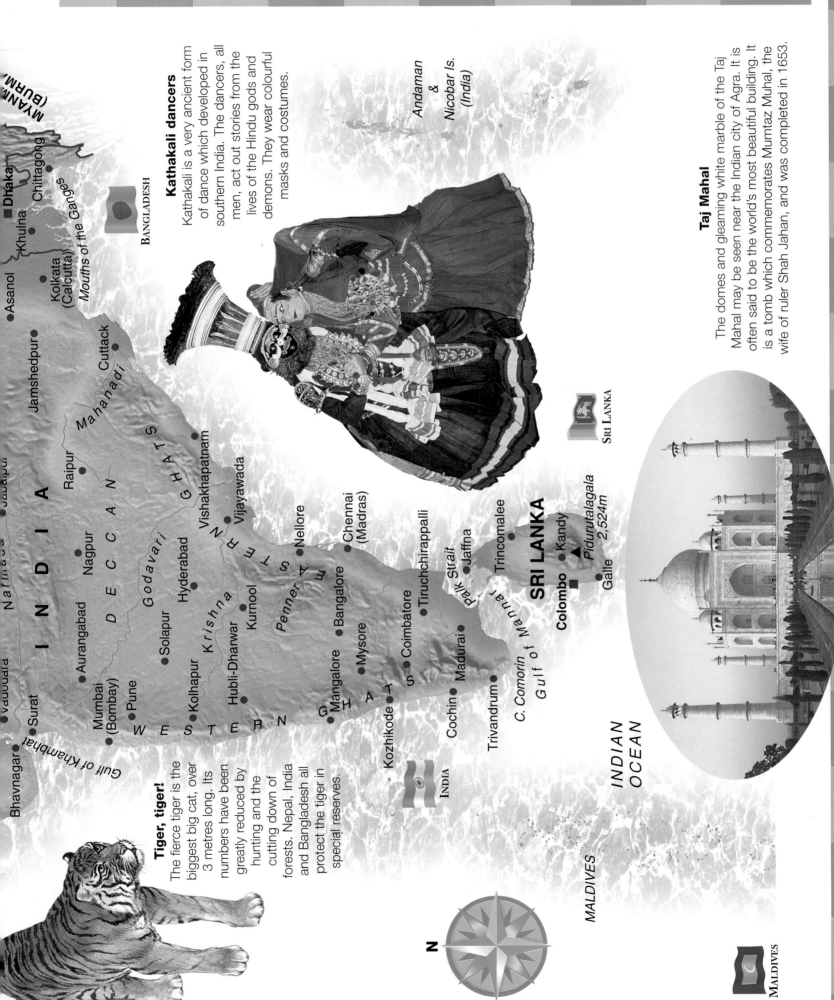

Fact Box

◆ Afghanistan
Area: 652,225 sq km
Population: 26,800,000
Official languages: Pushtu, Dari
Capital: Kabul
Currency: Afghani

◆ Bangladesh
Area: 144,000 sq km
Population: 131,300,000
Capital: Dhaka
Official language: Bengali
Currency: Taka

◆ Bhutan
Area: 46,620 sq km
Population: 800,000
Capital: Thimphu
Official languages: Dzongkha, English
Currency: Ngultrum

◆ India
Area: 3,166,830 sq km
Population: 1,029,000,000
Capital: Delhi
Official languages: Hindi, Assamese, Bengali, Gujarati, Kannarese, Kashmiri, Malayalam, Marathi, Oriya, Punjabi, Sanskrit, Sindhi, Tamil, Telugu, Urdu, Nepali
Currency: Indian rupee

◆ Maldives
Area: 298 sq km
Population: 300,000
Capital: Male
Official language: Divehi
Currency: Rufiyaa

◆ Nepal
Area: 141,415m sq km
Population: 25,200,000
Capital: Kathmandu
Official language: Nepali
Currency: Nepalese rupee

◆ Pakistan
Area: 803,940 sq km
Population: 144,600,000
Capital: Islamabad
Official language: Urdu
Currency: Pakistani rupee

◆ Sri Lanka
Area: 65,610 sq km
Population: 19,400,000
Capital: Colombo
Official language: Sinhalese, Tamil
Currency: Sri Lankan rupee

Kathakali dancers

Kathakali is a very ancient form of dance which developed in southern India. The dancers, all men, act out stories from the lives of the Hindu gods and demons. They wear colourful masks and costumes.

Taj Mahal

The domes and gleaming white marble of the Taj Mahal may be seen near the Indian city of Agra. It is often said to be the world's most beautiful building. It is a tomb which commemorates Mumtaz Muhal, the wife of ruler Shah Jahan, and was completed in 1653.

Tiger, tiger!

The fierce tiger is the biggest big cat, over 3 metres long. Its numbers have been greatly reduced by hunting and the cutting down of forests. Nepal, India and Bangladesh all protect the tiger in special reserves.

45

CHINA AND ITS NEIGHBOURS

CHINA is the world's third largest country in area, and has a higher population than any other. It is bordered by the world's highest mountains, by deserts and by tropical seas.

Most people live in the big industrial cities of the south and east and on the fertile plains around two great rivers, the Huang He and the Chang Jiang. Crops include wheat, maize, tea, sugar-cane and rice. Rice is eaten with almost every meal.

Chinese civilization dates back over thousands of years. Chinese inventions included paper and gunpowder and Chinese crafts included the making of fine porcelain and silk. Since 1949 China has been ruled by its Communist Party, making it the last big Communist nation, though its increasingly free economy is now one of the most important in the Pacific region. In 1997 it took back the territory of Hong Kong, an international centre of business which had been a British colony. China also claims the island of **Taiwan**, which is still governed independently by Chinese nationalists who lost power in 1949.

The **Korean peninsula** saw bitter fighting between 1950 and 1953, when Korea divided into two nations, North and South. These countries remain enemies today. South Korea has become an important industrial power.

Far to the north the Mongol peoples live in the independent republic of **Mongolia**. This includes the barren Gobi desert and remote grasslands.

KAZAKHSTAN
Ulaangom
Hovd
Fuhai
Karamay
ALTAI MTS.
Ebinur Hu
Yining
Kuytun
Dzungaria
KYRGYZSTAN
TIAN SHAN
Ürümqi
Hami
Aksu
Bosten Lake
Turfan Depress
Kashi
TAKLIMAKAN DESERT
ALTUN SHAN
Yur
▲Mt. K2
Hotan
KUNLUN SHAN
KARAKORAM
PLATEAU OF TIBET
INDIA
Siling Lake
TANGGULA S
Nam Lake
Tangra Lake
Lhasa
Mt. Everest 8,848 m
Xigaze
M
NEPAL
BHUTAN
A

The Great Wall
A defensive wall runs across the north of China for about 6,000 kilometres, with many extra twists and turns. It was started in about 246 BC and added to over hundreds of years.

Temple of Heaven
Tiantan, the Temple of Heaven in Beijing, is a beautiful group of buildings first raised in 1420. The Chinese emperors used to come here to pray for a good harvest.

Xinjiang herders
These herders are from Tangbula in Xinjiang, a remote region about the size of Alaska in China's far west. Xinjiang is home to several different peoples, including Uygurs, Kazakhs and Uzbekis.

FACT BOX
♦ **China**
Area: 9,597,000 sq km
Population: 1,275,000,000
Capital: Beijing
Main language: Standard Chinese
Currency: Yuan

♦ **Taiwan**
Area: 35,990 sq km
Population: 21,500,000
Capital: Taipei
Main language: Standard Chinese
Currency: New Taiwan dollar

♦ **North Korea**
Area: 122,310 sq km
Population: 24,400,000
Capital: Pyongyang
Main language: Korean
Currency: Won

♦ **South Korea**
Area: 98,445 sq km
Population: 45,900,000
Capital: Seoul
Main language: Korean
Currency: Won

♦ **Mongolia**
Area: 1,565,000 sq km
Population: 2,371,000
Capital: Ulan Bator
Official language: Mongolian
Currency: Tugrik

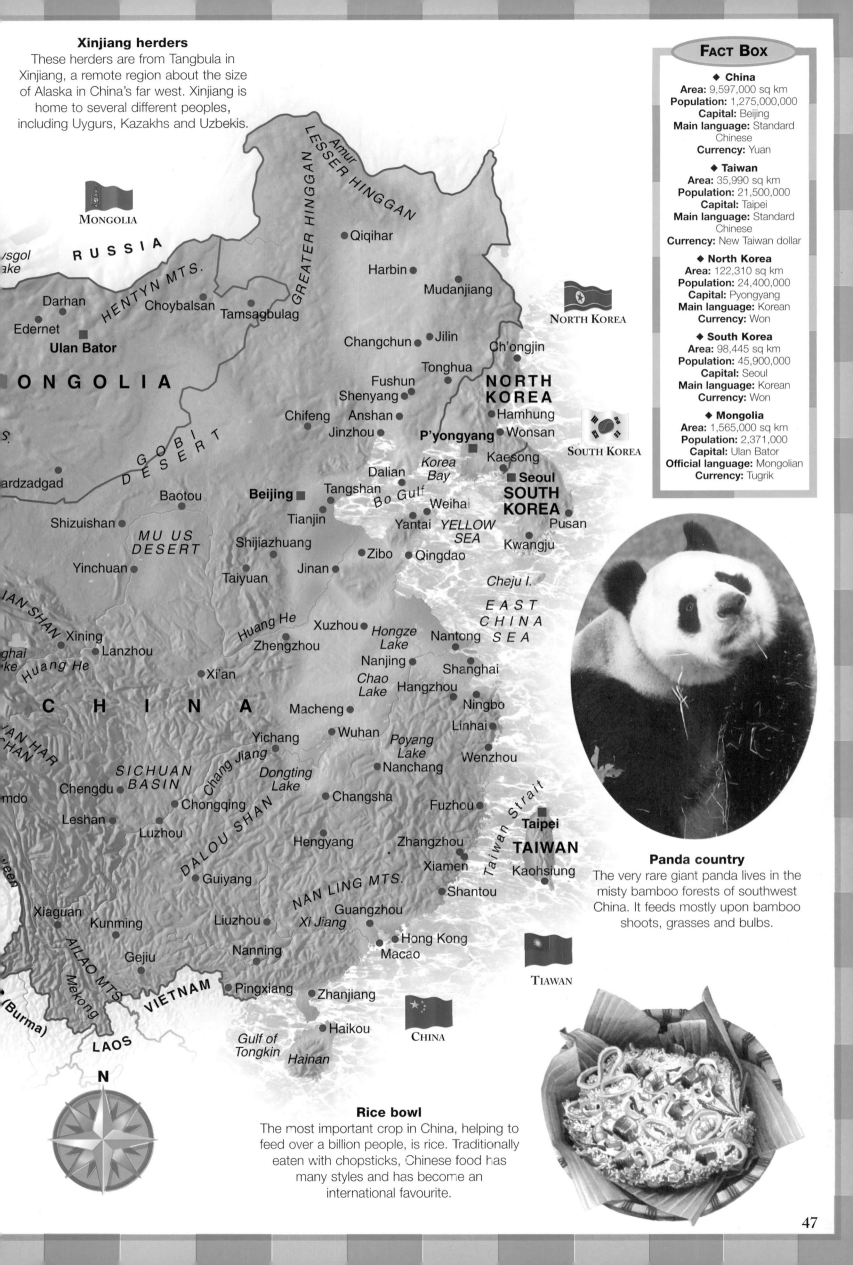

MONGOLIA

RUSSIA

Amur

LESSER HINGGAN
GREATER HINGGAN

HENTYN MTS.

Ysgol Lake

Darhan
Ederneet
Choybalsan
Tamsagbulag
Ulan Bator

MONGOLIA

Qiqihar
Harbin
Mudanjiang

Changchun · Jilin
Tonghua

NORTH KOREA

Ch'ongjin

NORTH KOREA

GOBI DESERT

ardzadgad
Baotou
Shizuishan

MU US DESERT

Yinchuan

Fushun
Shenyang
Chifeng Anshan
Jinzhou

Hamhung
P'yongyang · Wonsan
Kaesong

SOUTH KOREA

Dalian
Korea Bay

Beijing Tangshan
Tianjin Bo Gulf
Shijiazhuang
Taiyuan

Weihai
Yantai
Seoul
SOUTH KOREA
Pusan

AN SHAN
Xining
ghai
ke Lanzhou
Huang He

Zibo · Qingdao

Cheju I.

Huang He
Zhengzhou
Xi'an

Xuzhou
Hongze Lake
Nanjing
Chao Lake

Nantong

EAST CHINA SEA

CHINA

Macheng

AN HAR SHAN

mdo

SICHUAN BASIN
Chengdu

Leshan
Luzhou

DALOU SHAN

Chang Jiang
Dongting Lake
Chongqing

Yichang
· Wuhan
Poyang Lake
· Nanchang

Changsha

Hengyang

Shanghai
Hangzhou
Ningbo
Linhai
Wenzhou

Fuzhou

Taiwan Strait

Taipei
TAIWAN

Xiaguan
Kunming
Gejiu

Guiyang

Liuzhou

NAN LING MTS.
Guangzhou
Xi Jiang

Shantou

Xiamen
Kaohsiung

AILAO MTS
Mekong

(Burma)

VIETNAM

Nanning
Pingxiang

Hong Kong
Macao

Zhanjiang

TAIWAN

CHINA

LAOS

N

Gulf of Tongkin
Haikou
Hainan

Panda country
The very rare giant panda lives in the misty bamboo forests of southwest China. It feeds mostly upon bamboo shoots, grasses and bulbs.

Rice bowl
The most important crop in China, helping to feed over a billion people, is rice. Traditionally eaten with chopsticks, Chinese food has many styles and has become an international favourite.

JAPAN

JAPAN is made up of over 3,000 islands, and these stretch for about 3,000 kilometres from north to south on the northwest rim of the Pacific Ocean.

The chief islands are called Hokkaido, Honshu, Shikoku and Kyushu. The islands extend from the tropical south to the chilly north, where winter snowfalls can be heavy. The region is a danger zone for earthquakes and Japan's highest mountain, Fuji, is a volcano.

The snow-covered slopes of Mount Fuji have been a favourite subject for Japanese artists over the years. Japan has a long history of excellence in art, theatre, poetry, architecture and pottery. Japanese civilization dates back over 2,000 years. The country has been ruled by emperors and, during the Middle Ages, it was fought over by powerful warlords and bands of knights called samurai. Faiths include Buddhism and Shinto, the country's traditional religion.

Japan is very mountainous and so land that is suitable for farming is very precious. Japanese farmers grow rice, tea and fruit and the country also has a large fishing fleet. Many meals are based on rice or fish. Japan has very few natural resources. Even so, over the last 50 years Japan has become a leading world producer of cars, televisions and other electrical goods.

The mountains also limit the spread of housing and so Japan's cities are mostly crowded on to the strip of flat land around the coast. Tokyo has spread out to join up with neighbouring cities, and now has a population of over 25 million.

The Japanese people make up 99 percent of the country's population. The remainder includes Koreans and the Ainu of the far north, who may be descended from the first people to inhabit Japan.

Mount Fuji

The beautiful peak of Mount Fuji, to the southwest of Tokyo, is a national symbol and, traditionally, a sacred mountain.

Sushi

Prawns, raw fish, seaweed, pickles and vegetables are used to make these tasty snacks. Like most Japanese dishes, they are served with rice. Japanese food is often beautifully arranged and thoughtfully served.

Tea time

Tea is harvested on the inland slopes. The Japanese are great tea-drinkers and have an ancient ceremony at which tea is specially prepared and served.

FACT BOX

◆ **Japan**
Area: 369,700 sq km
Population: 127,000,000
Capital: Tokyo
Main language: Japanese
Currency: Yen

Kuril Is. (Russia)

JAPAN

La Pérouse Strait

Rebun I.
Rishiri I.
Wakkanai

Teshio

H o k k a i d o

Asahigawa
▲ Asahi/Mt.
2,290 m

Ishikari

Ishikari Bay
Otaru
Sapporo

Kushiro

Obihiro

Erimo Cape

Muroran

Uchiura Bay

Hakodate

Tsugaru Strait

Mutsa Bay

Hirosaki

Aomori

Hachinohe

Morioka

Kitak

Akita

S E A   O F   J A P A N

48

Itsukushima, Japan

Japan has many ancient Shinto shrines and Buddhist temples and many of these are set in beautiful scenery or gardens. Japan has always produced very simple and beautiful architecture and design.

Sumo wrestlers

The ancient sport of sumo is still very popular in Japan. Super heavyweight wrestlers aim to ground their opponents or force them out of the ring. There are long ceremonies before each contest.

Ride the Bullet

Japan's Bullet Train offers one of the world's most famous passenger express services. It speeds across the country, linking the capital, Tokyo, with other large cities.

A Shinto wedding

Dressed in her beautiful silk robe, or kimono, a Japanese bride sits next to her new husband, who also wears traditional costume. The wedding has been a Shinto ceremony. Shinto is an ancient Japanese faith which honours ancestors and the spirits of nature.

Sendai
Iwaki
Abukuma
Hitachi
Yamagata
Fukushima
Koriyama
Mito
Niigata
JAPAN
Chiba
Sado
Nagaoka
Utsunomiya
Tokyo
Yokohama
Toyama
Ueda
Takasaki
Kawasaki
Sagami Bay
Shinano
Matsumoto
Kofu
O-shima
Kanazawa
JAPANESE ALPS
Mt. Fuji 3,776 m
Shizuoka
Miyake I.
Fukui
Gifu
Toyota
Hamamatsu
Hachijo I.
Takefu
Biwa Lake
Nagoya
Matsusaka
PACIFIC OCEAN
Kyoto
Osaka
Sakai
Kobe
Wakayama
Oki Is.
Honshu
Kii Channel
Matsue
Okayama
Takamatsu
Shikoku
Hiroshima
Inland Sea
Tokushima
Matsuyama
Kochi
Tsushima
Suo Sea
Bungo Channel
Kitakyushu
Fukuoka
Sasebo
Omuta
Kumamoto
Kyushu
Nagasaki
Amakusa Is.
Sendai
Miyazaki
Koshiki Is.
Kagoshima
Tanega
Yaku

N

SOUTHEAST ASIA

SOUTHEAST ASIA is a region of forests and islands. **Myanmar (Burma)** lies between the hill country of India and China. It is crossed by the great Irrawaddy river, which flows south into the Indian Ocean. To the southeast is **Thailand**, a country green with rice fields and teak forests. To the west lie the lands once known as Indo-China – **Laos**, **Cambodia** and, on the long Mekong River, **Vietnam**.

Linked to the Asian mainland by a narrow isthmus, or strip of land, is **Malaysia**. This country also takes up the northern part of the island of Borneo, which it shares with the small oil-rich state of **Brunei**. Malaysia produces rubber, rice, tea and palm oil. Kuala Lumpur is a centre of international business, symbolized by the record-breaking Petronas Towers skyscrapers. **Singapore**, a small independent city state built on the islands across the Johor Strait, is another leader in the business world.

Indonesia is the world's largest island chain, with more than 13,600 islands. It includes Sumatra, Java, Bali and West Papua (the western half of New Guinea). Another large island chain, the **Philippines**, lies between the Pacific and the South China Sea.

All the islands bordering the Pacific Ocean lie in a danger zone for earthquakes and volcanoes. The region as a whole has a warm, often humid, climate, with monsoon winds bringing heavy rains. Southeast Asia's dwindling tropical forests are a last reserve for giant apes called orang-utans.

Many different peoples live in Southeast Asia, including Burmese, Vietnamese, Thais and Filippinos. There are also many people of Chinese and Indian descent. Buddhism is a major faith in the region. Most Indonesians are Muslims and most Filippinos are Roman Catholic. During the last 50 years Southeast Asia has been torn apart by wars. The region now looks forward to a period of peace.

The face of a demon
This fierce-looking demon guards the gate of the Grand Palace in Bangkok, the capital of Thailand. Many tourists come to this kingdom, once known as Siam, to see its ancient temples and enjoy its beautiful scenery and beaches.

A dome of gold
The fantastic roofs of Shwe Dagon pagoda shimmer with gold. This holy site is in Yangon, capital city of Myanmar (Burma). The pagoda honours Gautama Buddha, the founder of the Buddhist faith.

Javanese carving

These beautiful figures, carved from stone, decorate Borobodur on the island of Java. This 9th-century temple is the most splendid in Indonesia. Its carvings show scenes from the life of the Buddha.

PHILIPPINES

Laoag
Luzon
Mt. Pinatubo ▲
■ Manila
Mindoro

PHILIPPINES

Panay
Iloilo • Tacloban
Palawan • Cebu City
Negros Bohol

INDONESIA

BRUNEI

SULU SEA

Mindanao

Mt. Kinabalu
4,094 m ▲
Zamboanga • Davao
Bandar Seri Begawan
Mt. Apo
2,954 m
• Sandakan
SABAH

CELEBES SEA

EAST TIMOR

BRUNEI

RAWAK
puas
ORNEO • Balikpapan
Barito
Manado
MOLUCCA SEA

Halmahera

Floating market

At a Thai market, fruit, vegetables or fish may be sold from small boats. These women traders wear broad-brimmed straw hats to protect them from the tropical sun and the heavy monsoon rains.

Banjarmasin
I N D O N E S I A
• Palu
Sulawesi
Moluccas
Sorong
Jayapura

CERAM SEA
Seram
Buru • Ambon
WEST PAPUA
Puncak Jaya ▲
5,030m
NEW GUINEA

Ujung Pandang
Baubau
BANDA SEA
Aru Is.
Digul
PAPUA NEW GUINEA

E A
FLORES SEA
Wetar
Tanimbar Islands

N

Surabaya
Bali Lombok
alang Sumbawa
Flores
Dili
EAST TIMOR
Sumba Ende
Timor
• Kupang

Kuala Lumpur

High-rise buildings are influenced by traditional styles in Kuala Lumpur, capital of Malaysia. 'KL' is one of the most important centres of industry and business in Southeast Asia.

Komodo dragon

Meet the biggest lizard in the world, 3 metres long and weighing in at up to 136 kilograms. It is found on four small islands in Indonesia, called Rintja, Flores, Padar and Komodo.

51

NORTH AND WEST AFRICA

THE SAHARA IS THE WORLD'S LARGEST DESERT, made up of over 9 million square kilometres of baking hot sand, gravel and rock.

Its northern fringes, occupied by **Morocco**, **Algeria**, **Tunisia** and **Libya**, run into the milder, more fertile lands of the Mediterranean coast and the Atlas mountain ranges. They are home to Arabs and Berbers.

Deserts stretch from the Sahara eastwards to **Egypt** and the Red Sea. In ancient times one of the greatest civilizations the world has seen grew up in Egypt. Then as now, the country depended on water from the world's longest

Water for sale
A Berber water seller walks the streets of Marrakech, in Morocco, offering metal cups to passers-by.

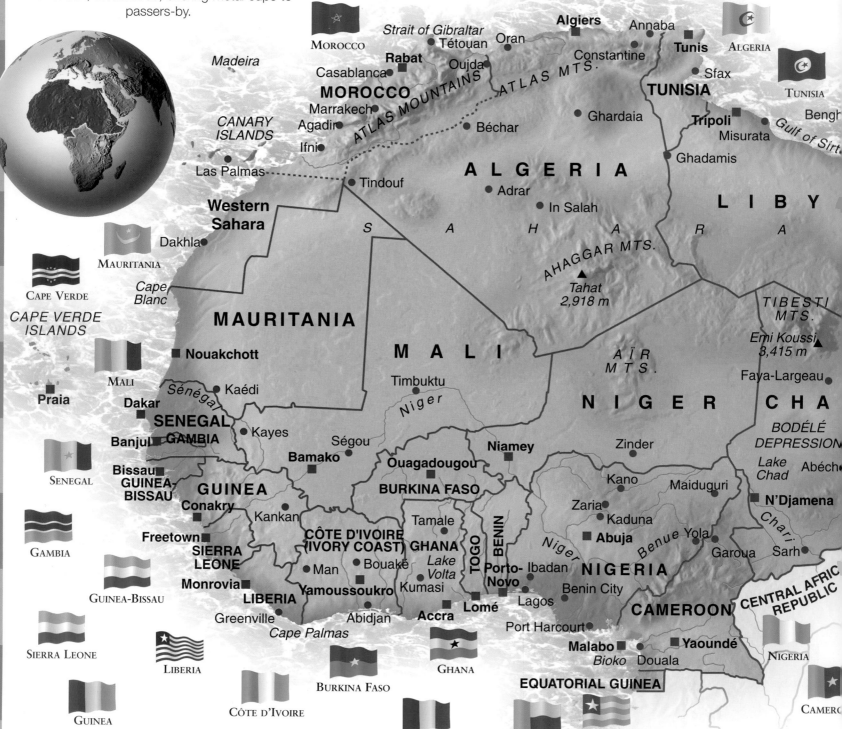

MOROCCO
Strait of Gibraltar
Tétouan
Oran
Algiers
Annaba
Tunis
ALGERIA
Rabat
Oujda
Constantine
Casablanca
MOROCCO
ATLAS MOUNTAINS
ATLAS MTS.
Sfax
TUNISIA
TUNISIA
Madeira
Marrakech
Ghardaia
Tripoli
Bengh
Agadir
Béchar
Misurata
Gulf of Sirt
CANARY
ISLANDS
Ifni
Ghadamis
Las Palmas
A L G E R I A
L I B Y
Tindouf
Adrar
In Salah
Western
Sahara
S
A
H
A
R
A
Dakhla
AHAGGAR MTS.
MAURITANIA
Tahat
2,918 m
TIBESTI
MTS.
Cape
Blanc
MAURITANIA
Emi Koussi
3,415 m
CAPE VERDE
ISLANDS
M A L I
AÏR
MTS.
Faya-Largeau
Nouakchott
Timbuktu
N I G E R
C H A
MALI
Sénégal
Kaédi
Niger
BODÉLÉ
DEPRESSION
Praia
Dakar
Kayes
Ségou
Niamey
Zinder
Lake
Chad
Abéche
SENEGAL
SENEGAL
Bamako
Ouagadougou
Kano
Maiduguri
Banjul GAMBIA
N'Djamena
Bissau
GUINEA-
BISSAU
GUINEA
BURKINA FASO
Zaria
Kaduna
Chari
GAMBIA
Conakry
Kankan
Tamale
Abuja
Yola
GUINEA-BISSAU
Freetown
CÔTE D'IVOIRE
(IVORY COAST)
GHANA
Niger
Garoua
Sarh
SIERRA
LEONE
Man
Bouaké
Lake
Volta
Porto-
Ibadan
NIGERIA
Monrovia
Yamoussoukro
Kumasi
Novo
Benin City
CENTRAL AFRIC
REPUBLIC
GUINEA-BISSAU
LIBERIA
Greenville
Abidjan
Accra
Lomé
Lagos
CAMEROON
SIERRA LEONE
Cape Palmas
Port Harcourt
NIGERIA
LIBERIA
Malabo
Yaoundé
Bioko
Douala
CÔTE D'IVOIRE
GHANA
BURKINA FASO
EQUATORIAL GUINEA
CAMERO
GUINEA
CHAD
BENIN
TOGO

52

river, the Nile. This flows north to the Mediterranean from the mountains of **Ethiopia** and the swamps of southern **Sudan**, Africa's largest country.

The region south of the Sahara is known as the Sahel. It includes **Senegal**, **Mauritania**, **Mali**, **Niger**, **Burkina Faso** and **Chad**. The people include the Fulani, Kanuri and Hausa. The thin grasslands of the Sahel allow cattle herding, but droughts are common and the desert is spreading. Many people are very poor.

Thirteen nations border the great bulge of the West African coast, around the Gulf of Guinea. The coastal strip is made up of lagoons and long sandy beaches fringed with palm trees. Inland there is a belt of forest, which rises to dry, sandy plateaus and semi-desert in the far north. West African history tells of African kingdoms and empires which grew up here long ago, but also of the cruel slave trade across the Atlantic, which lasted from the 1500s to the 1800s. In the 1800s, large areas of West Africa became colonies of Britain and France. Today these lands are independent. The region has rich resources, including oil and diamonds.

Abu Simbel
When the new Aswan dam was being built in the 1960s this great temple of the ancient Egyptian ruler Rameses II had to be moved stone-by-stone

FACT BOX

◆ Morocco
Area: 458,730 sq km
Population: 28,200,000
Capital: Rabat
Official language: Arabic
Currency: Dirham

◆ Western Sahara
Area: 252,120 sq km
Population: 261,000
disputed territory
Official language: Arabic
Currency: Dirham

◆ Algeria
Area: 2,381,745 sq km
Population: 29,800,000
Capital: Algiers
Official language: Arabic
Currency: Algerian dinar

◆ Tunisia
Area: 164,150 sq km
Population: 9,300,000
Capital: Tunis
Official language: Arabic
Currency: Tunisian dinar

◆ Libya
Area: 1,759,540 sq km
Population: 5,600,000
Capital: Tripoli
Official language: Arabic
Currency: Libyan dinar

◆ Egypt
Area: 1,000,250 sq km
Population: 64,800,000
Capital: Cairo
Official language: Arabic
Currency: Egyptian pound

◆ Sudan
Area: 2,505,815 sq km
Population: 28,129,000
Capital: Khartoum
Official language: Arabic
Currency: Sudanese pound

◆ Eritrea
Area: 91,600 sq km
Population: 3,500,000
Capital: Asmara
Languages: Tigrinya, Amharic
Currency: birr

◆ Ethiopia
Area: 1,104,300 sq km
Population: 58,700,000
Capital: Addis Ababa
Official language: Amharic
Currency: Birr

◆ Djibouti
Area: 23,200 sq km
Population: 600,000
Capital: Djibouti
Languages: Arabic, French
Currency: Djibouti franc

◆ Mauritania
Area: 1,030,700 sq km
Population: 2,400,000
Capital: Nouakchott
Languages: Arabic, French
Currency: Ouguiya

◆ Mali
Area: 1,240,140 sq km
Population: 10,137,000
Capital: Bamako
Official language: French
Currency: Franc CFA

◆ Burkina Faso
Area: 274,122 sq km
Population: 10,900,000
Capital: Ouagadougou
Official language: French
Currency: Franc CFA

◆ Niger
Area: 1,186,410 sq km
Population: 9,800,000
Capital: Niamey
Official language: French
Currency: Franc CFA

◆ Chad
Area: 1,284,000 sq km
Population: 7,000,000
Capital: N'Djamena
Languages: Arabic, French
Currency: Franc CFA

◆ Cameroon
Area: 475,500 sq km
Population: 13,900,000
Capital: Yaoundé
Languages: English, French
Currency: Franc CFA

◆ Equatorial Guinea
Area: 28,050 sq km
Population: 379,000
Capital: Malabo
Official language: Spanish
Currency: Franc CFA

◆ São Tomé and Príncipe
Area: 964 sq km
Population: 124,000
Capital: São Tomé
Official language: Portuguese
Currency: Dobra

◆ Nigeria
Area: 923,850 sq km
Population: 119,328,000
Capital: Abuja
Official language: English
Currency: Naira

◆ Benin
Area: 112,620 sq km
Population: 5,900,000
Capital: Porto-Novo
Official language: French
Currency: Franc CFA

◆ Togo
Area: 56,785 sq km
Population: 4,700,000
Capital: Lomé
Official language: French
Currency: Franc CFA

◆ Ghana
Area: 238,305 sq km
Population: 18,100,000
Capital: Accra
Official language: English
Currency: Cedi

◆ Côte d'Ivoire
Area: 322,465 sq km
Population: 15,000,000
Capital: Abidjan
Official language: French
Currency: Franc CFA

◆ Liberia
Area: 111,370 sq km
Population: 2,640,000
Capital: Monrovia
Official language: English
Currency: Liberian dollar

•Sierra Leone
Area: 72,325 sq km
Population: 4,494,000
Capital: Freetown
Official language: English
Currency: Leone

◆ Guinea
Area: 245,855 sq km
Population: 7,500,000
Capital: Conakry
Official language: French
Currency: Guinean franc

◆ Guinea-Bissau
Area: 36,125 sq km
Population: 1,028,000
Capital: Bissau
Official language: Portuguese
Currency: Guinea-Bissau peso

◆ Gambia
Area: 10,690 sq km
Population: 1,200,000
Capital: Banjul
Official language: English
Currency: Dalasi

◆ Senegal
Area: 196,720 sq km
Population: 8,800,000
Capital: Dakar
Official language: French
Currency: Franc CFA

◆ Cape Verde Islands
Area: 4,035 sq km
Population: 395,000
Capital: Praia
Official language: Portuguese
Currency: Cape Verde escudo

LIBYA

Darnah

Alexandria · Port Said
· Suez
QATTARA Cairo ■
DEPRESSION Sinai Pen.

Asyût ·
· Qena
E G Y P T
Lake · Aswân
Nasser

EGYPT

N

Nubian Desert
Port Sudan ·

Merowe ·

· Atbara

S U D A N
Kassala ERITREA
Omdurman ■ Asmara

Khartoum ■

▲ Jabal Marrah El Obeid ·
3,088
Kosti ·

· Aksum
ETHIOPIAN
Lake · Gonder
Tana PLATEAU
Debre Markos ·

Addis Ababa ■

SUDD Gore ·
ETHIOPIA Ogaden
Webe Shebele

RED SEA

ERITREA

DJIBOUTI
■ Djibouti

DIJBOUTI

RIFT VALLEY

SOMALIA

Nimule ·

UGANDA KENYA

CHAD

SUDAN

ETHIOPIA

CENTRAL, EASTERN & SOUTHERN AFRICA

CENTRAL AFRICA is dominated by the river Congo, which flows through hot and humid rainforest to the Atlantic Ocean. The great river winds through the **Democratic Republic of the Congo**, and the network of waterways which drain into it provide useful transport routes for riverboats and canoes.

A long crack in the Earth's crust, the Great Rift Valley, runs all the way down **East Africa**. Its route is marked by volcanoes and lakes. Some East African mountains remain snow-capped all year round, even though they are on the Equator. The highest of these is Kilimanjaro, at 5,950 metres. It looks out over savanna, grasslands dotted with trees. Huge herds of wildlife roam these plains. Zebra, giraffe, elephants and lions are protected within national parks. The Indian Ocean coast includes white beaches and coral islands. Mombasa, Dar-es-Salaam and Maputo are major ports.

In southern Africa the Drakensberg mountains descend to grassland known as veld. There are harsh deserts too, the Kalahari and the Namib. The **Republic of South Africa** is one of the most powerful countries in Africa. It has ports at Durban and Cape Town.

Central and southern Africa are rich in mineral resources, including gold, diamonds and copper. Eastern and southern Africa are important farming regions, raising cattle and producing coffee, vegetables, tropical fruits, tobacco, and grape vines.

African kingdoms flourished in the Congo region in the Middle Ages and the stone ruins of Great Zimbabwe recall gold traders of long ago. Today the region is home to hundreds of African peoples with many different languages and cultures.

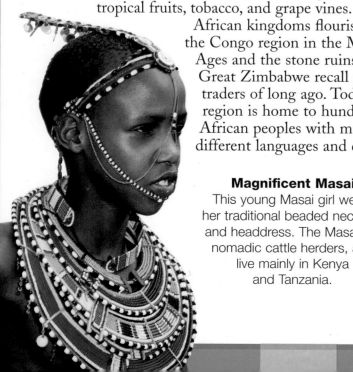

Magnificent Masai
This young Masai girl wears her traditional beaded necklace and headdress. The Masai are nomadic cattle herders, and live mainly in Kenya and Tanzania.

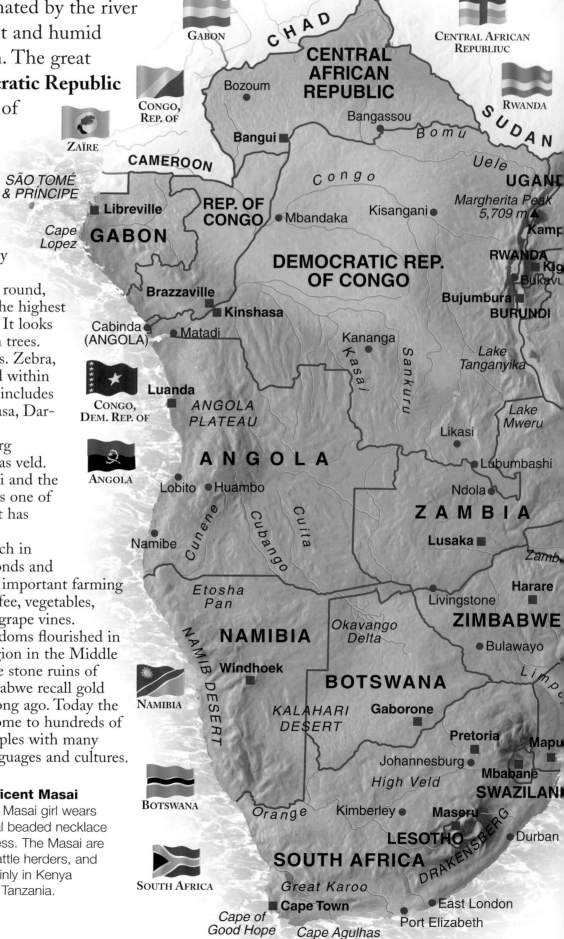

GABON

CENTRAL AFRICAN REPUBLIUC

CONGO, REP. OF

RWANDA

ZAÏRE

SÃO TOMÉ & PRÍNCIPE

CONGO, DEM. REP. OF

ANGOLA

NAMIBIA

BOTSWANA

SOUTH AFRICA

CHAD

CENTRAL AFRICAN REPUBLIC

Bozoum

Bangassou

Bangui

Bomu

Uele

SUDAN

CAMEROON

Congo

UGAND

Kisangani

Margherita Peak 5,709 m ▲

Kamp

Libreville

REP. OF CONGO

Mbandaka

RWANDA

Cape Lopez

GABON

DEMOCRATIC REP. OF CONGO

Kig
Bukavu

Brazzaville

Bujumbura

BURUNDI

Kinshasa

Cabinda (ANGOLA)

Matadi

Kananga

Kasai

Sankuru

Lake Tanganyika

Luanda

ANGOLA PLATEAU

Lake Mweru

Likasi

Lubumbashi

A N G O L A

Ndola

Z A M B I A

Lobito • Huambo

Zamb

Namibe

Cunene

Cubango

Cuita

Lusaka

Harare

Etosha Pan

Livingstone

ZIMBABWE

NAMIBIA

Okavango Delta

Bulawayo

Windhoek

Limpo

BOTSWANA

KALAHARI DESERT

Gaborone

Pretoria

Johannesburg

Mapu

High Veld

Mbabane

SWAZILAN

Orange

Kimberley

Maseru

LESOTHO

DRAKENSBERG

SOUTH AFRICA

Durban

Great Karoo

Cape Town

East London

Cape of Good Hope

Cape Agulhas

Port Elizabeth

La Digue, Seychelles
Over 100 islands make up the Seychelles. La Digue is only 15 square kilometres in area, but the third most populated.

Cape Caseyr

● Berbera

SOMALIA

KENYA

UGANDA

ETHIOPIA

Lake
Turkana

KENYA

Juba

N

Kisumu   Mt. Kenya
▲5,199 m

Mogadishu

ake
toria   ■ Nairobi

Tana

● Kismayu

INDIAN OCEAN

anza

▲
Kilimanjaro
5,895 m

● Mombasa

BURUNDI

SOMALIA

SEYCHELLES

SEYCHELLES

odoma

● Zanzibar
● Dar-es-Salaam

ANZANIA

Rufiji

Aldabra Is.

MALAWI

Lake
Nyasa

C. Delgado

COMOROS

C. d'Ambre

ALAWI

ongwe

Antisiranana

MADAGASCAR

● Moçambique

Mozambique Channel

Mahajanga

● Blantyre

Toamasina

MOZAMBIQUE

MAURITIUS

eira

Antananarivo

ZAMBIA

MADAGASCAR

MAURITIUS

MOZAMBIQUE

Fianarantsoa

Réunion
(France)

ZIMBABWE

C. Ste. Marie

Sting in the tail
A scorpion's curled-forward tail contains a sting that can be deadly. Scorpions are most common in desert areas.

SWAZILAND

LESOTHO

55

AUSTRALIA

THIS COUNTRY is the size of a continent, a huge mass of land surrounded by ocean. The heart of **Australia** is a vast expanse of baking desert, salt pans, shimmering plains and dry scrubland. Ancient, rounded rocks glow in the morning and evening sun.

These barren lands are fringed by grasslands, tropical forests, creeks and fertile farmland. In the far east is the Great Dividing Range, which rises to the high peaks of the Australian Alps. The southeast is crossed by the Murray and Darling rivers. The Great Barrier Reef, the world's largest coral reef, stretches for over 2,000 kilometres off the eastern coast, while the island of Tasmania lies to the south across the Bass Strait.

Most Australians don't live in the 'outback', the dusty back country with its huge sheep and cattle stations and its mines. They live in big coastal cities such as Brisbane, Sydney, Adelaide and Perth. There they enjoy a high standard of living, an outdoor lifestyle, sunshine and surfing.

To the many people who in recent years have come from Europe and Asia to settle in Australia, this seems like a new country. However it is really a very ancient land, cut off from other parts of the world so long that it has many animals seen nowhere else on Earth, such as kangaroos, echidnas and platypuses.

Australia has probably been home to Aboriginal peoples for over 50,000 years. European settlement began in 1788, when the British founded a prison colony at Botany Bay, near today's city of Sydney. Many Australians still like to keep in touch with British relatives and traditions, but the modern country follows its own path as one of the great economic powers of the Pacific region.

Opera on the harbour
Sydney's most famous landmark is its Opera House, built between 1959 and 1973. It rises from the blue waters of the harbour like a great sailing ship. Sydney, the capital of New South Wales, is Australia's biggest city with a population of about 3,700,000.

Christmas beetles
Australia and its surrounding islands are populated by many weird and wonderful insects and beetles. These beetles are from Christmas Island.

Aboriginal art
An Aboriginal artist from Groote Eylandt, an island in the Gulf of Carpentaria, completes a painting on bark. Paintings by Australia's Aborigines are admired around the world. They often recall the ancient myths and legends of their people, with bold, swirling patterns or pictures of animals.

Bonapart Archipel
Broome
Fitzroy
Eighty Mile Beach
Port Hedland
De Grey
Barrow I.
Fortescue
Ashburton
Mt. Bruce
GIBSON DESERT
Lake Macleod
Carnarvon
Murchison
Dirk Hartog I.
WESTERN AUSTRALIA
Laverton
Geraldton
Kalgoorlie-Boulder
Perth
Fremantle
Bunbury
C. Naturaliste
Archipelago of the Recherche
C. Leeuwin
Albany

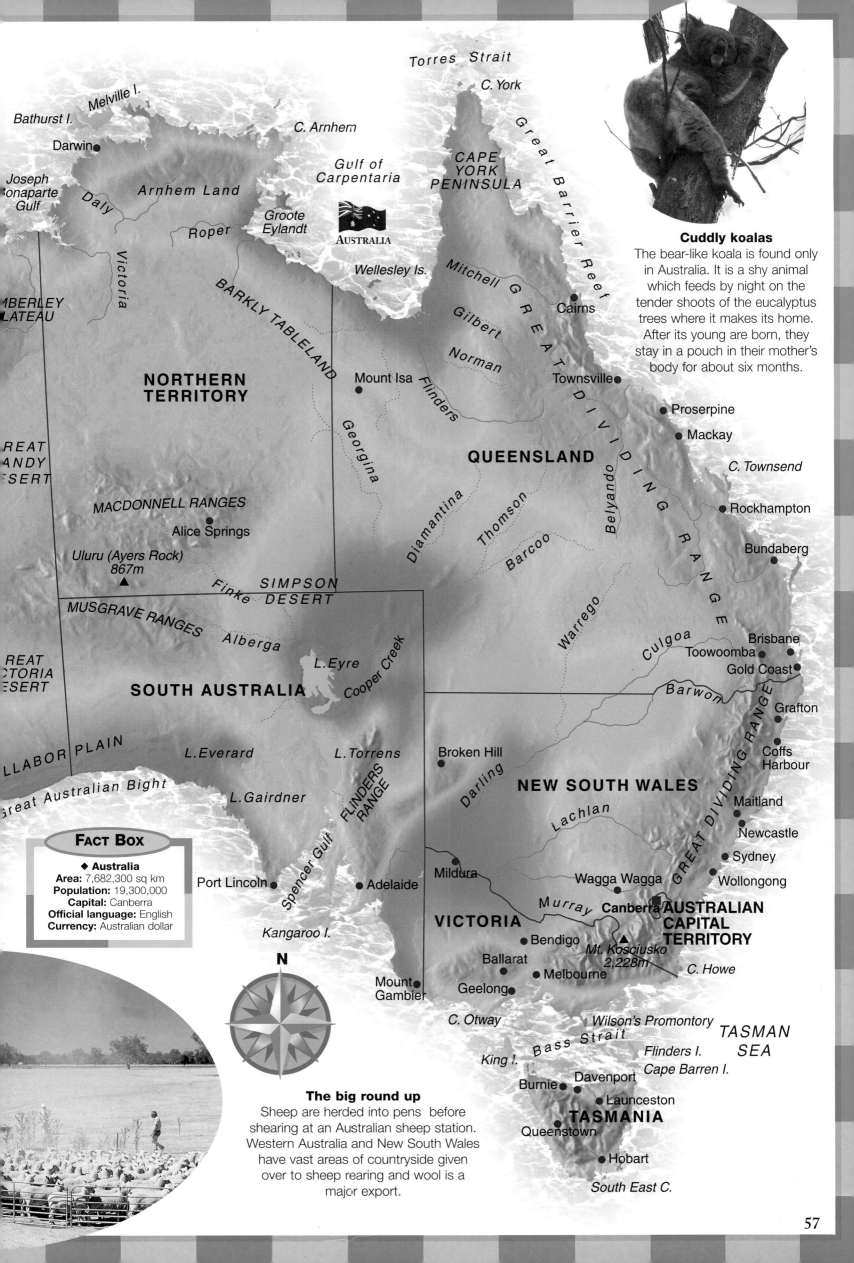

Torres Strait

C. York

Melville I.

Bathurst I.

Darwin

Joseph Bonaparte Gulf

C. Arnhem

Daly

Arnhem Land

Roper

Gulf of Carpentaria

Groote Eylandt

Wellesley Is.

AUSTRALIA

CAPE YORK PENINSULA

Great Barrier Reef

Mitchell

Gilbert

Norman

Cairns

Cuddly koalas
The bear-like koala is found only in Australia. It is a shy animal which feeds by night on the tender shoots of the eucalyptus trees where it makes its home. After its young are born, they stay in a pouch in their mother's body for about six months.

KIMBERLEY PLATEAU

Victoria

BARKLY TABLELAND

NORTHERN TERRITORY

Georgina

Mount Isa

Flinders

QUEENSLAND

G R E A T

D I V I D I N G

R A N G E

Townsville

Proserpine

Mackay

C. Townsend

GREAT SANDY DESERT

MACDONNELL RANGES

Alice Springs

Uluru (Ayers Rock) 867m ▲

Finke

SIMPSON DESERT

Thomson

Belyando

Diamantina

Barcoo

Rockhampton

Bundaberg

MUSGRAVE RANGES

Alberga

L.Eyre

Cooper Creek

Warrego

GREAT VICTORIA DESERT

SOUTH AUSTRALIA

Culgoa

Toowoomba

Brisbane

Gold Coast

Barwon

Grafton

NULLABOR PLAIN

L.Everard

L.Torrens

FLINDERS RANGE

Broken Hill

Darling

NEW SOUTH WALES

Coffs Harbour

L.Gairdner

Lachlan

Maitland

Newcastle

Great Australian Bight

FACT BOX

◆ **Australia**
Area: 7,682,300 sq km
Population: 19,300,000
Capital: Canberra
Official language: English
Currency: Australian dollar

Spencer Gulf

Port Lincoln

Adelaide

Mildura

Wagga Wagga

Sydney

Wollongong

Murray

Canberra

AUSTRALIAN CAPITAL TERRITORY

VICTORIA

Bendigo

Mt. Kosciusko 2,228m ▲

C. Howe

Kangaroo I.

Ballarat

Melbourne

Geelong

N

Mount Gambier

C. Otway

Wilson's Promontory

TASMAN

King I.

Bass Strait

Flinders I.

Cape Barren I.

SEA

Burnie

Davenport

Launceston

The big round up
Sheep are herded into pens before shearing at an Australian sheep station. Western Australia and New South Wales have vast areas of countryside given over to sheep rearing and wool is a major export.

TASMANIA

Queenstown

Hobart

South East C.

NEW ZEALAND AND THE PACIFIC

NEW ZEALAND LIES in the Pacific Ocean, about 1,600 kilometres to the east of Australia. It has a moist, mild climate and many unusual plants, birds and animals may be found there.

Most of its people live on North Island and South Island. These beautiful islands, divided by the Cook Strait, are the largest of several which are included within the country. North Island has volcanoes, hot springs and gushing geysers. South Island is dominated by the peaks and glaciers of the Southern Alps. It also has deep sea inlets called fiords and rolling grassy plains. New Zealand, with its sheep, cattle and fruit farms, has one of the most important economies in the Pacific region.

Papua New Guinea is another island nation, bordering Indonesian territory on the island of New Guinea. It also includes several chains of smaller islands. Many of its mountain regions, blanketed in tropical forests, were only opened up to the outside world in the 20th century. The country is rich in mineral resources and its fertile soils produce coffee, tea and rubber.

Strung out eastwards across the lonely Pacific Ocean are many scattered island chains and reefs. Small coral islands surround peaceful blue lagoons ringed with palm trees. The islanders may make their living by fishing, growing coconuts, mining or tourism. Many of the island groups have banded together to form independent nation states.

Peoples of the Pacific are of varied descent. Some are the descendants of European settlers - for example the British in New Zealand, or the French on New Caledonia or Tahiti. Fiji has a large population of Indian descent. The original peoples of the Pacific fall into three main groups. Melanesians, such as the Solomon Islanders, live in the western Pacific, while Micronesians live in the Caroline and Marshall Islands. The Polynesian peoples, brilliant seafarers, colonized vast areas of the oceans, from New Zealand to the Hawaiian Islands. The Maoris, who make up nine percent of New Zealand's population, are a Polynesian people who have kept and valued many of their ancient traditions.

SEA OF JAPAN

MICRONESIA

Yellow Sea

East China Sea

SOLOMON ISLANDS

Northern Mariana Islands (USA)

SOUTH CHINA SEA

Guam (USA)

Federated States of Micronesia

Palau

Celebes Sea

Philippine Sea

Papua New Guinea

West Papua (Indonesia)

Arafura Sea

Port Moresby

Solomon Islands

Coral Sea

AUSTRALIA

TASMAN SEA

New Guinea finery
Feathers and paint are worn by many young warriors at tribal gatherings and feasts in remote areas of Papua New Guinea. The country has a very rich culture with over 860 different languages.

Kiwi fruit
When farmers decided to grow this fruit in New Zealand, they decided to give it a local name to help sales. The kiwi is the national bird, and a nickname for a New Zealander.

BERING SEA

PAPUA NEW
GUINEA

PALAU

N O R T H
P A C I F I C
O C E A N

Midway Island
(USA)

Wake Island
(USA)

MARSHALL
ISLANDS

Hawaii (USA)

VANUATU

Marshall Islands

KIRIBATI

Nauru   NAURU

Kiribati

Tuvalu

TUVALU

SAMOA

Galapagos
(Ecuador)

S O U T H
P A C I F I C
O C E A N

anuatu   **Samoa**   American
                        Samoa

Fiji

ew Caledonia
(France)

Cook Islands
(New Zealand)

French
Polynesia

Pitcairn Island
(UK)

Easter Island
(Chile)

NEW ZEALAND

Tonga

FIJI

TONGA

**NEW
ZEALAND**

Easter Island
Hundreds of huge,
mysterious stone
heads tower above the
hills of Easter Island, in
the eastern Pacific.
They were erected by
Polynesians about
1,000 years ago. Today
Easter Island is
governed by Chile.

◆ **Papua New Guinea**
Area: 462,840 sq km
Population: 4,400,000
Capital: Port Moresby
Official language: English
Currency: Kina

◆ **New Zealand**
Area: 265,150 sq km
Population: 3,600,000
Capital: Wellington
Official language: English
Currency: New Zealand dollar

◆ **Palau**
Area: 490 sq km
Population: 16,000
Capital: Koror
Official languages: Palauan,
English
Currency: US dollar

◆ **Marshall Islands**
Area: 181 sq km
Population: 52,000
Capital: Majuro
Official languages: Marshallese,
English
Currency: US dollar

◆ **Solomon Islands**
Area: 29,790 sq km
Population: 354,000
Capital: Honiara
Official language: English
Currency: Solomon Islands
dollar

◆ **Tuvalu**
Area: 25 sq km
Population: 13,000
Capital: Funafuti
Official languages: Tuvaluan,
English
Currency: Australian dollar

◆ **Kiribati**
Area: 684 sq km
Population: 75,000
Capital: Bairiki
Official language: English
Currency: Australian dollar

◆ **Nauru**
Area: 21 sq km
Population: 10,000
Capital: Yaren
Official language: Nauruan
Currency: Australian dollar

◆ **Fiji**
Area: 18,330 sq km
Population: 758,000
Capital: Suva
Official language: English
Currency: Fiji dollar

◆ **Tonga**
Area: 699 sq km
Population: 103,000
Capital: Nukualofa
Official languages: Tongan,
English
Currency: Pa'anga

◆ **Vanuatu**
Area: 14,765 sq km
Population: 156,000
Capital: Porta-Vila
Official languages: Bislama,
English, French
Currency: Vatu

◆ **Samoa**
Area: 2,840 sq km
Population: 170,000
Capital: Apia
Official languages: Samoan,
English
Currency: Tala

◆ **Federated States of
Micronesia**
Area: 702 sq km
Population: 114,000
Capital: Palikir
Official language: English
Currency: US dollar

NEW ZEALAND

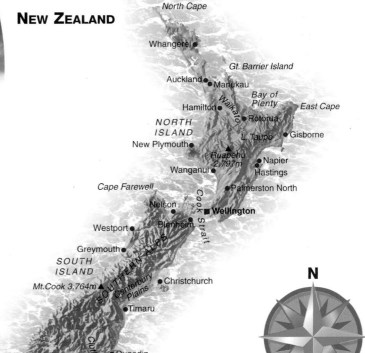

North Cape

Whangerei

Gt. Barrier Island

Auckland Manukau

Bay of
Plenty

Hamilton   East Cape

NORTH   Rotorua
ISLAND

L. Taupo   Gisborne

New Plymouth

Ruapehu
2,797m   Napier

Wanganui   Hastings

Cape Farewell   Palmerston North

Nelson

Cook Strait

Westport   **Wellington**

Blenheim

Greymouth

SOUTH
ISLAND

Canterbury
Plains

Mt.Cook 3,764m   Christchurch

SOUTHERN ALPS

Timaru

Clutha

Dunedin

Foveaux Strait Invercargill

Stewart Island

N

Gusher!
Steam bursts from volcanic
rocks near Rotorua on
North Island. New
Zealand's geysers and hot
springs are not just a
tourist attraction. They are
used to generate electricity.

POLAR LANDS

THE NORTHERNMOST PART of our globe is called the Arctic. Within this bitterly cold region lie the northern borders of Alaska (part of the United States), Canada, Greenland, Norway, Sweden, Finland and Russia.

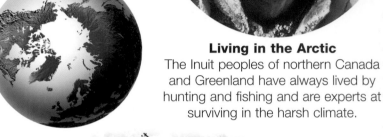

Living in the Arctic
The Inuit peoples of northern Canada and Greenland have always lived by hunting and fishing and are experts at surviving in the harsh climate.

The huge island of **Greenland**, or Kalaalit Nunaat, is a self-governing territory of Denmark, with a population of just 57,000. Its peoples are descended from both Inuit and Scandinavians.

Most of the Arctic region is covered by the Arctic Ocean, much of which is frozen solid all year round. At the centre of this great cap of ice is the North Pole. The **Arctic** supports diverse wildlife, including seals, walruses and polar bears. Peoples who have learned to live permanently in the far north include the Aleuts, the Inuit, the Saami, the Yakuts and the Chukchi. They have been joined in recent years by workers from the oil industry.

The only people to be found in **Antarctica**, at the other end of the globe, are scientists studying the weather and rocks of the coldest and windiest continent on Earth. The only other living things to survive here are the penguins which breed around the coast and the whales, birds and fishes of the Southern Ocean. The landmass is ringed by a shelf of ice, some of which breaks away to form massive icebergs in the spring. Inland there are mountain ranges and icy plains. The Antarctic winter takes place during the Arctic summer, and the Antarctic summer during the Arctic winter.

Various countries claim territory in Antarctica, and the continent is rich in minerals and fishing. However many scientists argue that this land should never be opened up to mining and industry, but left as the planet's last true wilderness.

Antarctic melt
Each southern spring, the ice around Antarctica begins to melt, allowing ships to approach the ice shelves around this huge, frozen continent.

FACT BOX

◆ **Arctic Circle**
Area of ocean:
14,056,000 sq km

◆ **Antarctic Circle**
Area of land:
13,900,000 sq km

The publishers wish to thank the artists who have contributed to this book:
Julie Banyard; Martin Camm; Mike Foster; Josephine Martin; Terry Riley; Guy Smith; Roger Smith; Michael White/Temple Rogers.

The publishers would like to thank the following for supplying photographs for the Atlas

Page 5 (T/R) MKP; 5 (B) PhotoDisc; 6-7, 9, 10-11 all MKP; 12 (C/R) & (B/L) Spectrum Colour Library; 14 (T/R) MKP; (B/L) & (B) The Stock Market; 15 (B) MKP; 17 (C/R) & B/R) The Stock Market; (B) MKP; 18 (B) MKP; (T/R) & (B/R) The Stock Market; 20-21, 24-25 all MKP; 26 (T/C) MKP; (B/C) The Stock Market; 28 (B/C) The Stock Market; 29 (T/R) The Stock Market; 30 both MKP; 32-33 (C) MKP; 33 (C) The Stock Market; 33 (B/R); MKP; 34 (T/L) MKP; 34 (B) The Stock Market; 35 (C) MKP; 37 (T/L) The Stock Market; (B/C) PhotoDisc; 38 (B/L) MKP; 39 (T/R) PhotoDisc; (C) & (B/R) The Stock Market; 40-41 all Sue Cunningham Photographic; 42-43 all MKP; 44 (T/L) MKP; 45 (C/R) The Stock Market; (B) MKP; 46 (T/R) The Stock Market; (B) & (B/C) MKP; 47 (C/R) MKP; 48 (T/R) & (C) MKP; 49 (C/R) MKP; (B/C) The Stock Market; 50-51 all MKP; 52-53 all MKP; 54-55 all The Stock Market; 56 (T/R) & (B/L) MKP; (B/C) The Stock Market; 58-59, 60-61 all MKP